M000282112

Matt McMillen is a bestselling Christian author and teacher of God's Word. His books and massive social media ministry has taught countless amounts of people their true identity in Christ. Matt's easy-to-understand biblical teachings have helped build confidence in his readers, break lifelong addictions, and find their true purpose for living: enjoying God's grace through Jesus Christ!

For more information on his ministry, visit:
www.mattmcmillenministries.com

THE CHRISTIAN IDENTITY

VOLUME 3

Discovering What Jesus Has Truly Done to Us

MATT MCMILLEN

The Christian Identity, Volume 3
Discovering What Jesus Has Truly Done to Us

Published by: Matt McMillen Ministries
720 W. Karsch Blvd.
Farmington, MO 63640
matt@mattmcmillen.com

First Printing, 2019

Printed in the United States of America

ISBN 978-0-9971533-6-1 (paperback)

For my father-in-law, Phil. Thank you for always being so kind to me. You've impacted my life in a wonderful way. I'll be forever grateful for you.

Contents

"All over the world this gospel is bearing fruit and growing, just as it has been doing among you since the day you heard it and truly understood the grace of God."

Colossians 1:6

Introduction

Who Are You, Christian?

Jesus, once more deeply moved, came to the tomb. It was a cave with a stone laid across the entrance. "Take away the stone," he said.

"But, Lord," said Martha, the sister of the dead man, "by this time there is a bad odor, for he has been there four days."

Then Jesus said, "Did I not tell you that if you believe, you will see the glory of God?"

So they took away the stone. Then Jesus looked up and said, "Father, I thank you that you have heard me. I knew that you always hear me, but I said this for the benefit of the people standing here, that they may believe that you sent me."

When he had said this, Jesus called in a loud voice, "Lazarus, come out!" The dead man came out, his hands and feet wrapped with strips of linen, and a cloth around his face.

Jesus said to them, "Take off the grave clothes and let him go." (John 11:38-44)

An entire book could be written about this incredible portion of Scripture, but for a moment, let's picture them walking down the road away from the tomb...

Lazarus, with eyes wide open clears his throat, "**cough* *cough*...* Wow! That was *insane*! Here I was, hanging out with Moses and Abraham—Jonah and Job were there too—and boom! I'm stumbling out of my tomb right back here with you!"

"Heaven is pretty amazing, isn't it?" Jesus replies.

"Yes Lord, it is!"

"And Lazarus?"

"Yeah, Jesus?"

"I thought I asked you to take those grave clothes off."

"What? These strips of linen? Well I pulled them off my face, is that not enough? The rest is so soft and comfortable. I think I'll keep them on."

"But you were dead," Jesus retorts, "you're not dead any longer. It's not proper for someone who isn't deceased to wear that. In fact, it's weird."

"What do you mean?"

"I gave you life and those grave clothes don't fit."

"Ah, I get it, Jesus. I see what you're saying and that makes sense!"

Immediately Lazarus begins grasping all over his body, pulling off piece by piece this outfit which represents death. Finally free and continuing on, he asks, "So Jesus?"

"Yes, Laz?"

"When were you going to tell us about Krispy Kremes?"

Grave clothes? I said to myself as I sat staring at the page.

In my mid-30s, as I grew in the truths of the New Covenant, many Bible stories started to have new meanings. Since I understood the context—based on what Christ brought in through His death and resurrection—the account of Lazarus coming back to life wearing a dead man's attire really stood out.

Grave clothes?... Grave clothes! Jesus is talking about Lazarus' former identity as a corpse! Why didn't I see this before?!

It was as if I was reading a whole new Bible, but I wasn't! I was simply having my mind renewed by the Spirit of Jesus within me. He was teaching me what this meant, as well as hundreds of new things, based on *His* accomplishments.

Sitting in my big chair, feet up on the ottoman and pondering what I now knew, I'm sure those grave clothes were soft as soft could be. All wrapped up nearly swaddled, I bet they felt good! But it looked *strange* for a living person to wear grave clothes. This is why Jesus said to take them off.

Unfortunately, 2,000 years later we Christians do the same thing when we "wear" dead people's apparel after being brought back to life by our Savior:

- **False humility?** This looks weird. We don't need to insult ourselves to appear holy. Holy is what we *are*.
- **Sinning?** Always looks weird. We don't *want* to sin because we're new creations who have the sinless nature of God. Anything that's not of faith isn't natural.
- **Using the Law for guidance?** Weird. We don't need the Law because we have something so much better, God's very Spirit living within! *He* guides us moment by moment, not 613 all-or-nothing commandments.
- **Judging whether or not someone is saved?** Very weird. No matter what a person's life looks like, nothing can override the power of the Father and Son's promise made to each other at the Cross. We *know* if someone has believed in their promise for forgiveness, once, they've accessed God and God's unbreakable oath. We know, because this happened to *us* by grace through faith.

- **Refusing to forgive others?** This is extremely weird. Forgiveness is part of our spiritual DNA because God poured Himself into our very being. We're new creations in Christ, so when we deny someone forgiveness we're denying who we are. His Spirit even teaches us we can forgive and still set healthy boundaries to protect ourselves from harm.

Oh there's more! Lots and lots more! That's exactly what we'll get to in this book! I'm so excited you've decided to join me in the final volume of *The Christian Identity Series*!

As you read, if you have any questions don't hesitate to reach out to me at matt@mattmcmillen.com. Every devotional in this book is available for free on my website. If you'd like to share them on social media, email to a friend, or print some out, please do! My web address is: www.mattmcmillen.com.

Lastly, please read one day at a time and don't skip ahead. As you spend a full month with me we'll dive deeper into how to spot dead people's grave clothes—the stuff that doesn't fit! As a believer, Christ has called you out of your tomb and given you His life!

Let's do a closet clean-out in your mind of everything which doesn't belong to a resurrected child of God.

That's you, dear Christian. That's your identity.

Day 1

Surrounded by a Great Cloud of Witnesses

"Therefore, since we are surrounded by such a great cloud of witnesses, let us throw off every encumbrance and the sin that so easily entangles, and let us run with endurance the race set out for us. Let us fix our eyes on Jesus, the author and perfecter of our faith, who for the joy set before Him endured the cross, scorning its shame, and sat down at the right hand of the throne of God."

Hebrews 12:1-2

I miss my grandma a lot. She graduated into her heavenly body in December of 2018. Since then, the only way I can hear her voice is to replay messages I've got saved on my phone, or through a couple Facebook videos. Her voice was like no other. From the time I was a baby, then a teenager, and on into adulthood, hearing Grandma always brought a sense of relief to my mind. During her last months on earth she deteriorated rather quickly, yet her voice stayed the same:

> "What do you mean leave a message and you'll call me back. This is your grandmother and I used to change your dirty, stinky diapers. I love you. Call me back when you get a chance, darlin.'"
>
> "Come here, baby. Let Grandma pray for you."
>
> "I'm so proud of you, Son. If those foster parents who treated you so poorly could only see you now, my oh my. They'd be shocked."
>
> "Matthew, God's grace is always sufficient for you. It really is. Just lean into it and things will get better, you'll see."

So many phrases and conversations I can recall. The things she taught me by example, such as forgiveness, compassion, empathy, and seeing everyone through the eyes of Jesus, meant so much. I *really* miss Grandma. I'd like to talk to her but I know she's enjoying her best life.

There's a passage in the Bible, in Hebrews, where the author talks about a great cloud of witnesses surrounding us, as if we're being watched by those who've died and gone to heaven. I'd like to think Grandma is doing this somehow, looking down on me, but I don't see that as true. I believe she's involved in such an uninterrupted glory with God that what's happening here on earth isn't her focus. She's in the timeless realm, and I'm still here, finishing my journey.

And you know what? I'm fine with that. She ran her race of grace for 89 years and now she's fully immersed in what was beyond the finish line, the reward of the inheritance. Hallelujah, hallelujah, and hallelujah!

Since I've grown in the truths of the New Covenant, I've learned the great cloud of witnesses in Hebrews 12 isn't dead relatives peeking in on us. To get the context, first we must understand what the author was trying to accomplish by writing this letter to the Hebrews. He, or she, was trying to make a big deal of Jesus to the Jews—the Hebrews—who refused to believe Christ was their Messiah.

The Jews held angels and prophets in high esteem, so in chapters 1 and 2 the writer explains how Jesus is greater than both. This person does the same thing in chapter 3, pointing out the supremacy of Jesus to Moses. Also, in chapter 3, a giant elephant in the room is introduced. The only unforgivable sin: REJECTING BELIEF IN CHRIST AS SAVIOR.

On and on the author lays out Jesus' eminence compared to fallible human priests, Levi, Abraham, and even Melchizedek.

"NOBODY HAS SUCH POWER!" was the message to the Hebrews, "BELIEVE HIM!"

In essence, he or she was pleading with the Law-loving Jews, "Please! Don't shrink back toward the Law! It is a shadow and Christ is making that shadow with Himself! There's no more sacrifice left to be found at the temple! Don't wander in the desert of unbelief like your ancestors! BELIEVE GOD ABOUT JESUS! Rest in the finished work of Messiah and drink in God's grace! Your earthly temple cannot compare to the heavenly temple! Your animal blood cannot compare to the blood of Jesus! Repent of your unbelief because there will be severe punishment for those who reject Him!"

We Christians don't have to worry about any of that stuff. Why not? Because we've already believed. He will return for us without reference to any of our sins (see Hebrews 9:28).

As we work our way to chapter 11 we find out who's in the great cloud of witnesses. It's those who believed God and lived before Christ came; a list of people who were justified by faith before the Cross. They longed for what we now have on this side of Calvary! As they patiently waited they never got to see Jesus but they still had a one-time saving faith! The author is making the point, "These people were great because of their faith, because they *believed* God, so you should too. But now, believe Him about Jesus."

They had to begin to view Christ as the One their scriptures pointed to. He's the only way they'd ever see their beloved patriarchs and matriarchs.

So today, my friends, know this: If you want to see your believing loved ones again, believe too, if you haven't. Today can be your day of salvation. If you've lost someone close to you, someone who's trusted Jesus at least once in their lifetime, you'll get to see them again! Our finite human minds can't comprehend what the saints are enjoying! You too are a saint, dear Christian! You too will be there before you know it!

A prayer for you: *Father, would you please say hi to Grandma for me. Tell her how much I love her and miss her. Tell her that Jennifer and Grace are doing well and that we all look forward to our reunion one day. Right now, I lift up all who are reading this, directly to you. For those who've lost someone special, remind them that our life here is just a blip on the radar of eternity. Because of Jesus, we believers will all meet again! It will be a magnificent day! And Dad, please reveal how powerful Jesus is. Expose His authority in the minds of those who doubt. What He did at the Cross, and through His resurrection, open up the true context of Scripture to those who are struggling with trusting Him. Amen.*

Day 2

Christians Should Always Be Themselves

"Therefore if anyone is in Christ, he is a new creation. The old has passed away. Behold, the new has come!"

2 Corinthians 5:17

"Don't be yourself! Be like Christ! There's many reasons why you *shouldn't* want to be yourself!"

This person yelling at me is extremely serious. Frustrated, it seems, but very stern. *They* do *not* want Christians to be themselves, and me advising us to do so has knocked over a hornet's nest.

But why? Why is this individual so upset about me saying we should be *exactly* who God has remade us to be? Why are they mad about me pointing out the truth, that we should always be ourselves? The answer is quite simple: *They don't know who they truly are as a Christian.*

Because of what they've been taught, legalistic roots, false humility, and even self-hate run deep in their minds. Not in *them* but in their minds. It takes time to till such up and haul it away as debris. They've been instructed to not trust themselves, to not like themselves, and most of all, to not be themselves.

Due to double-talk teaching—"Come to Jesus and be made new, just believe!"—but then, "Repent! You backslidden sinner! You will burn in hell for this!" they think God has baited and switched them; that He's saved them but not really. They're confused and confusion breeds irritation and anger. The freshly-saved Christian, new-car-smell believer, they want to hang onto so badly. But to achieve this it's contingent on *them* staying at battle with themselves. So how dare I say they should *be* themselves?

"Wrong, Matt! We need to be like Pastor and not like ourselves! You better seek wise counsel and study yourself approved! We should *never* be ourselves! Ever! We should always be striving to be more like Christ every single day!"

This is sad, but not far-fetched. Look at it this way, imagine if you yelled at a newborn baby, "You better be like your dad or else! You better prove you belong as a member of this family or you're out! You better get to work and study to find out how you should live your life! Never be yourself!"

Christians are treated this way all the time. We've not been taught the truth, that we've *already* been remade exactly like Christ. No more striving is necessary:

> *"Therefore if anyone is in Christ, he is a new creation. The old has passed away. Behold, the new has come!"* (2 Corinthians 5:17)

You are in Christ, Christian. That's what happened the moment you realized He forgave you. He placed you inside of Himself (see Galatians 3:2, Ephesians 1:13, Colossians 3:3, 1 Corinthians 6:17, John 14:20). But first, He made you just like Him:

"In this way, love has been perfected among us, so that we may have confidence on the day of judgment; for in this world we are just like Him." (1 John 4:17)

You're still in this world, dear believer, are you not? This identity passage is talking about now! You're just like Jesus! This is why you should always be yourself!

"Yeah right, Matt! The Bible is clear that we can walk according to the flesh!"

Friend, I know that, but a walk is not an identity. It's a walk. Further, what many believers don't understand is that the flesh is not *us*. When we begin to think of our physical body as the flesh—don't. This is where many fall off course, in thinking *the flesh* is our flesh, skin, and bone; our body. It's not.

The flesh is the power of sin coming to life *through* us but it's *not* us. The original Greek word is sarx and sarx doesn't mean physical flesh nor does it mean sinful nature. It simply means *the flesh*. We don't have an English translation which is accurate for sarx. For this reason we have to trust the Spirit in order to grasp the flesh's full meaning based on the context around it.

I have colleagues who call the flesh, "A way of getting fulfillment apart from Christ, apart from who we are," and I agree. The flesh can be debaucherous, legalistic, or even philanthropic. It's not simply drinking to excess, sleeping around, skipping church and partying hard—as the legalist claims. The flesh can appear as *good* by religious and worldly standards. It's anything—or our focus on any*one*—in which we're trying to find status other than who we already are.

Unless you're an unbeliever you're not *in* the flesh, even when you act like it. When you do it's just that, an act, a walk. As Paul listed off examples of living in the flesh for himself, he spoke of his past life as the best Mosaic legalist ever, a supreme religious man. This revealed that religion is the flesh too (see Philippians 3:4-9).

Ultimately, to describe the flesh, this is what matters most: *We are not the flesh.* As children of God, that's the bottom line. We *have flesh* but we are not *the* flesh. The flesh is the foreign object of sin, hamartia—a parasite which entered our physical realm through Adam (see Romans 5:12)—expressing itself through our members; our hands, feet, mouth, and even brain, creating sinful actions and thoughts (see Romans 7:23).

Paul's sinful thoughts were religious and covetous (see Romans 7:8). Many of my sinful thoughts were alcoholic, pornographic, self-abasing, and overly-competitive. The power of sin—hamartia—still presents such to me at times but I choose to not let the flesh come to life. I choose to not *walk* that way, to walk according to the flesh. How? By being myself!

Sin is in us—in our physical being—because we still live on this fallen planet, but sin is *not* us, as Christians. We've been taken out of the realm of the flesh—sin—and placed *in* Jesus (see Romans 8:9). We've been saved from sin completely because sin separates us from God (see Hebrews 7:25). Our one-time faith in the Cross accomplished this feat because the Cross dealt with the sin of the world *once* (see 1 John 2:2, 2 Corinthians 5:20-21, Hebrews 10:10).

Anytime you see the word *flesh* in Scripture look around it. Is it referring to your body? If so, then this is not what you are supposed to be fighting, as many teach. Paul said we are to care for our bodies not fight them (see Ephesians 5:29). Truthfully, even *the* flesh you shouldn't be fighting. I'll explain in a moment, but please know that your physical body is just as holy as your spirit and soul. All of you is blameless, Christian—spirit, soul, *and* body. Paul informed the Thessalonian believers of this truth (see 1 Thessalonians 5:23). He also told the Corinthians the same, that their bodies were temples of God! (See 1 Corinthians 6:19). God cannot live in unholy places, so guess what your body is? It's perfect! Your flesh is an exact fit—100% sanctified—for the Creator of the universe to dwell!

So remember, you are not the flesh but you *are* flesh. Separate these two when you read Scripture. Pause and look at the context. This will help you greatly in understanding the new creation you truly are!

When you know you're not the flesh, you can begin to comprehend another paramount truth: *Christians are never instructed to fight the flesh. The Spirit fights the flesh while we rest.*

At no point in the Bible are we advised to go to war with the flesh. Bad teaching says otherwise and the devil loves this because it causes self-hate and sometimes insanity. Aggression then ensues toward those who say to just be yourself. When we commingle the definitions of *flesh* and *the flesh* many interpret passages about the Spirit fighting the flesh and think *they too* have to fight the flesh. Oh no, not at all! We are called to back off *out* of that fight:

> *"For the flesh desires what is contrary to the Spirit, and the Spirit what is contrary to the flesh. They are in conflict with each other, so that you are not to do whatever you want."* (Galatians 5:17)

Do you see that? Who's at battle here? Who has the different set of desires? The flesh and the Spirit! Where are you, Christian? Are you in this fight? No! But when you try to get into it what happens? You *don't* do what you really want to do! Why? Because you're trying to do the Spirit's job!

The person who struggles with legalism and doesn't understand the flesh sees this passage one way, the New Covenant believer sees it completely different! The legalist thinks if we don't fight the flesh then, "You can just do whatever you want! All that nasty sinnin'!"

But no! That's not the context! When *those two* are fighting—the flesh and the Spirit—and we are resting, we are being ourselves and doing *exactly* what we want! Is it sinning? NO! We don't want to sin! *Sin* wants to sin not you!

Paul explained this to the Romans as he recounted his past life of fighting the flesh as a sanctimonious Pharisee:

"As it is, it is no longer <u>I myself who do it</u>, but <u>it is sin</u> living in me." (Romans 7:17)

What does it look like when we rest and don't fight? When we refuse to give sin an outlet through Mosaic commandment following or self-made commandment following?

"Love, joy, peace, patience, kindness, goodness, faithfulness, gentleness and self-control" (see Galatians 5:22-23)

None of these characteristics can be legislated! They are natural expressions of those who belong to Christ!

"Those who belong to Christ Jesus <u>have crucified the flesh</u> with <u>its</u> passions and desires. Since <u>we live by the Spirit</u>, let us keep in step with the Spirit." (Galatians 5:24-25)

Is this not exciting?! Yeah, it is!

In our efforts to do the Spirit's job—fight the flesh—we *won't* do what we truly want to do which is live by the Spirit, which is keeping in step with Him... walking. Therefore, what do we do? Rest. Be ourselves. Be God's child and express our true nature, God's own *divine* nature which we received in full the moment we placed our faith in Jesus (see 2 Peter 1:4, John 1:12-13, Colossians 1:22, 2:9-10).

So today, my friends, know this: Don't fake being yourself. Why would God make you new just so you can "act" new. Instead, *be* yourself. If you don't be yourself and express your heavenly nature, the world misses out on you. You've got too much to offer to not be you!

A prayer for you: *Heavenly Father, thank you for teaching me that I am not the flesh. Thank you for teaching me that my body is not the flesh—it's flesh. This biblical revelation changed so much for me! I was finally able to separate who I am from the power of sin being a barnacle, a leech, a tumor—but NOT me. Thank you! Right now, I lift up all who are reading this, directly to you. For those who've been taught they have a good dog and a bad dog inside them—to feed one and starve the other—give them relief today. Let them know, as your child, they don't have a bad dog. They don't have any dog. They have themselves. They are holy, blameless, new creations, forever connected to you and sealed up with your Spirit. There's no need to attempt to starve something within them that's not there. They simply need to learn more about who they are, and then be. They possess all they need for life and godliness. The work you began in their mind about this holiness of theirs, you are surely going to complete. Amen.*

Day 3

Christmas: The Beginning of a Great Union

"For to us a child is born, to us a son is given, and the government will be on his shoulders. And he will be called Wonderful Counselor, Mighty God, Everlasting Father, Prince of Peace."

Isaiah 9:6, penned 700+ years before Jesus was born

**Written Christmas morning, 2019*

Merry Christmas everyone! Although Jesus wasn't literally born on this date, today is the day we celebrate His birth! The enemy wants people to focus on Christmas having pagan roots. But in all actuality, missionaries world-wide used countless local customs in foreign cultures to teach people about Jesus; to find commonality. Why? To turn them from darkness to light (see Acts 26:18).

So what matters most? *God's Son was born and if we believe in Him we will have eternal life—His life! (See John 3:16, 10:28-30, Colossians 3:4).* Who cares if today was not the actual day? We can still celebrate!

Jesus came for both the Jew and the Gentile, to create a brand new union, a unique family! Paul told the Galatians Christ was born under the Law to redeem those who were under the Law (see Galatians 4:4-5). Who was under the Law? Only the Jews. We Gentiles were never given the Law (see Romans 2:14, Ephesians 2:12). Some have hijacked it and acted as if it's theirs, even today, but it never has been.

Currently, the Jews who don't believe Christ was their Messiah, wail at an old wall, begging God to hurry up and send a savior. But the wailing is over! The *wait* is over! Christ has come!

Although the Word decided to manifest Himself as a Jew (see John 1:1), the good news is He didn't *just* come for the Jews. He also came for us Gentiles! A Gentile is anyone on this planet who isn't a Jew—Jesus was born for us too!

The dividing wall of hostility, which Jesus tore down, the one Paul mentioned in Ephesians 2:14, was the Law:

"For He Himself is our peace, who has made the two one and has torn down the dividing wall of hostility"

The Law of Moses is that barrier! 613 commandments, not just ten! IT IS OBSOLETE FOR ALL WHO WILL BELIEVE CHRIST DIED FOR THEM! To be clear, it's still handy for those who don't believe. Its only use, just like from the time it was written, is to show a Law-lover's need for grace... for Jesus... for a better way (see John 14:6, Hebrews 7:19, 8:13, 1 Timothy 1:7-11, Romans 5:20, 6:14, Galatians 3:12,21).

The two becoming one, from Ephesians 2:14, was the Jew and the Gentile. When Christ said, "Blessed is the peacemaker," He's telling His Jewish audience they'd have to make peace with us (see Matthew 5:9). To them, we were aggressive heathens; low-life, dirty rotten Gentiles who never had the privilege of carrying God's oracles. We were considered dogs and pigs, not righteous like those who "obeyed" the Law (see Romans 3:2, Matthew 7:6). But Jesus gave us the opportunity at a great union through Himself!

So now, the Jew and the Gentile, the Jew and the Greek, the American, Ethiopian, Russian, Mexican, Iranian—everyone on planet earth—WE ARE ONE THROUGH CHRIST! ONE BODY WITH ONE HEAD! JESUS! His birth didn't bring in the New Covenant but His death *did* bring it to pass! (See John 19:30, Galatians 3:28, Hebrews 2:14-15, 9:16-18, 10:9, 1 Corinthians 12:12-27, Romans 12:4-5).

So today, my friends, know this: After Jesus was born, and when He gave His blood thirty-three years later, He didn't make us non-Jews, Jews. He completely removed our race—as well as the Jews'—and gave us both a new lineage: CHILD OF GOD. Through faith in Him there's neither Jew nor Gentile! We're a new creation all together! We are family! (See John 1:12-13, Galatians 6:15, 2 Corinthians 5:17).

A prayer for you: *Father, thank you for Jesus. And Jesus, thank you for coming to earth. We are so grateful for you! Thank you for giving us hope in a life with you! Right now, I lift up all who are reading this, directly to you. Because of the holidays, so many of these dear readers are in pain, please comfort them. Let them know you're there. Ease their minds about whatever they're worried about or feeling. Remind them you care deeply about what's hurting them. But also, many are enjoying today! They're enjoying you and their families! Only through Jesus can we do such a thing*

in the most authentic way possible. We can choose to forgive and love, and to let you live through us! We're so grateful for your life, your death, and your life after death! We're grateful for you bringing the world together! Amen!

Day 4

How Tithing Has Been Incorrectly Taught

"For God so loved the world, that He gave His only begotten Son, that whoever believes in Him shall not perish, but have eternal life."

John 3:16

"You can't afford *not* to tithe!"

This is a lie from someone who sees God as a graceless, merciless, two-faced, give-to-get deity. Even if they won't admit it, this is how they're painting our Heavenly Father. It's lies like these which confuse a lot of Christians, and plainly stated, makes the world hate us even more. It's not the gospel. It's not Jesus. It's aggressive, pressure-filled, twisted garbage—no different than pagan tribal religions.

It's just plain wrong but it's coming from self-proclaimed Christians. I'm not saying they *aren't* Christians, I'm saying their theology isn't biblical.

The truth is, tithing was grain, not cash for church members, in the passage from Malachi 3. Yes, the tithe was more than simply grain, it was animals and spices too, but in Malachi 3, grain is the context. That's why it says *storehouse* as this is where grain was stored. Also in Malachi 3, the *floodgates being opened* was rain for crops, not financial success. That's why it says there will be no room to store it. Store what? Grain. Grain needs water. God provides rain. *Floodgates* for rain come from the sky. God controls the sky, and rain. Therefore, give your grain to the Levites and stop robbing God.

This go-to chapter for the "tithing principle" was about storing grain so the Levitical priests could have food. They weren't allowed to work so this was how they ate. People tithed food to the priests from the tribe of Levi. Malachi was delivering God's message to Jewish people who were struggling with greediness.

Context matters. This wasn't directed at New Covenant believers. We are Christians. We live after the Cross. We are not Jews under the Mosaic Law. The Jews would laugh at us for even reading the Law. We were not invited. We were outsiders. They viewed non-Jews, Gentiles, as pigs and dogs who were unworthy of Law observance (see Ephesians 2:12, Matthew 7:6).

What's more, if someone wants to use the Law to establish a number to give, there were *three* types of tithing not just one, which equaled close to 23%, not simply 10% (see Numbers 18:21-26, Deuteronomy 14:22-27, 14:28-29).

Tithing was, and is, a matter of the Law. The Law is still in full force for unbelievers, but not for believers (see Matthew 5:17-19, 1 Timothy 1:6-11). Christians are not under the Law because we've believed in Jesus (see Galatians 2:19, 3:12, Romans 6:14, 7:4).

There are only two mentions of the tithe in the New Testament. Neither are commanding a Christian to give 10% nor an offering above a mandated 10%. Here are both:

1. **Luke 11:42, Matthew 23:23.** This is the same event written through the perspective of two different people. Both Luke and Matt are

referring to food, not money for a church. The first church *building* wasn't even erected until approximately 200 years after Christ. So "giving to your church, and/or ministry of choice" is off base. In these passages, Jesus is chewing out self-righteous Pharisees for neglecting weightier matters *of the Law*. What does that tell us? Tithing is included with the Mosaic Law. And again, Christians are not under the Law (see previous passages, as well as 2 Corinthians 3). This is before the Cross and Jesus is speaking to Jews under the Law. This is not a commandment for a Christian to tithe. We cannot use this passage for such because such is not the context. Start from the beginning of the chapter, read down, and it's clear to see who Jesus is barking at—legalists who say, "Look at how much I give."

2. **Hebrews 7.** Abraham is mentioned tithing a tenth of his *spoils of war* to a priest named Melchizedek, who appeared before the Law was established. This is not cash, check, or credit to a church, but booty from a plunder. It's people's stuff Abraham took after a battle, not food, not money. Melchizedek was an early appearance of Christ in the Old Testament, more than likely (see Genesis 14). This chapter, Hebrews 7, is saying Jesus is greater than the Levites because the Levitical priests came from Levi, and Levi came from the loins of Abraham. Abraham tithed Melchizedek, honoring him. Law, which is represented by Levi, honored grace by honoring Melchizedek with the tithe. Jesus *is* grace (see John 1:17). Grace is represented in this mystery priest because he had no human lineage like Abraham did. Therefore the New Covenant is greater than the Old Covenant. Grace is greater than Law. Read all of Hebrews 7 to see this. Hebrews is written to the Jews—the *Hebrews*—not us Gentiles, like the other letters such as Ephesians, Romans, Corinthians, Colossians, and more. Gentiles were never given the Law, so the author of this book never

> had to unsell us from what was established in the Torah, the first five books of the Bible. The Jews were stuck on what Moses wrote and refused to believe in Christ as Messiah. This chapter has nothing to do with a Christian tithing. It's a comparison for the Hebrew people to see Jesus as the greatest person ever. Why? So they would repent from believing in all of their religious patriarchs and turn to believing in Christ.

So, that's it. No more references of tithing in the entire New Testament. Don't you think that if tithing was so important, Paul, James, John, Peter, Jude—*any* apostle—would have mentioned it when writing their epistles? Yet it is completely absent.

Am I saying don't tithe? No, that's not what I'm saying. I'm saying let's not put a number on our giving. Let's remove the word tithe because that's a number and God isn't looking for a number.

Give, don't tithe.

Our churches will survive and they'll survive for the right reasons.

I'm saying what Paul said, "Give freely, from the heart, *not* under pressure" (see 2 Corinthians 9:7). The tithing pressure doesn't work anyway. It only creates fear and anxiety, or hypocrisy, none of which are from God. The reality is, most don't tithe and those who *give* don't give a full 10% (see Church Giving Statistics, July 2018).

I've also heard, "The tithe is just the beginning for New Covenant believers, we are to give *more* than 10%." This is not true. Such would make the New Covenant more stringent than the Old, which had 613 regulations to follow perfectly in order to be blessed perfectly (see Deuteronomy 4:2, Matthew 5:48).

We can't do this. That is, make Christ a slot machine by creating New Covenant Law.

Friends, we don't give to get. We don't give to be blessed. We don't give because a really good salesman on stage says God will give us a promised return on our investment. We don't give because a person is going crazy on stage either, sweating profusely, or telling us about *their* success from giving. Giving ROI testimonials are nearly demonic (videos of success from tithing shown before the tithe is asked for). God isn't pleased with them. His blessings can't be bought.

Nor do we give because the person up front is nice, gentle, and calm while explaining how God will give success *back* to you *through* your giving. This creates just as much pressure as the guy with the sweat-rag. Some people deliver pressure in a berserk way, some in a smooth way, some in a funny and entertaining way, and others in a passive-aggressive way. It's *all* pressure the same. Pressure is a red flag for Christians to pause. It was for freedom that Christ set us free and pressure takes our freedom away, momentarily, in our minds (see John 8:36, Galatians 5:1).

One last thing. Tithing does not break any curses. That threat by pastors must stop. Tithing is a matter of the Law and Christ took on the full curse of the Law in Himself so that *we believers* could be free from any curses (see Galatians 3:10-13). Children of God cannot be cursed. It's impossible because of the Cross. In fact, we've been blessed with *every* spiritual blessing in Christ Jesus (see Ephesians 1:3).

So today, my friends, know this: We *give,* not tithe, because we are giving people at heart, because we have new hearts—hearts like God. By having the same heart of God we are natural givers because He is the greatest giver ever (see Ezekiel 36:26, Romans 6:6-10, 2 Corinthians 5:17, 2 Peter 1:4, John 3:16).

A prayer for you: *Father, thank you for everything you've given me. It's like Grandma used to say, "All good things come from above." I know that's true, but even deeper, you aren't above me, you are in me. Thank you for giving me your Spirit. I am so wealthy I don't know what to do with all the blessings, of you. Right now, I lift up all who are reading this, directly to you. For a lot of them, they've been taught they need to give you money so they can enjoy you giving more money back to them. I ask for you to mature their understanding of just how great and gracious you are. It is you who wants to continually give, freely, and in Christ you've given us the most precious gift of all time. He's worth more than anything in the universe and beyond what we can see in our physical realm. We're so grateful for your Son. Thank you. Amen.*

Day 5

The Truth About Hebrews 10:26

"If we deliberately keep on sinning after we have received the knowledge of the truth, no sacrifice for sins is left"

Hebrews 10:26

Hebrews 10:26 is a scary passage *if* we don't understand who it is written to and why. What makes this section of Scripture even more terrifying is when we read the next verse out of context, right along with it. From a twisted perspective—which would be applying Hebrews 10:26 and 27 to Christians—we can expect some bad stuff from God. The person who struggles with sanctimoniousness will say if we deliberately keep on sinning we should have:

"a fearful expectation of judgment and of raging fire that will consume the enemies of God." (See Hebrews 10:27)

Friend, let me ease your mind. This is not directed at believers but only toward those who had heard the message about Jesus and refused to believe. They listened to the apostles' information but were stonewalling at admitting Christ was the final sacrifice for sins. They tasted the gospel but never swallowed, therefore making a mockery of the Son of God (see Hebrews 6:4-6).

The book of Hebrews is called Hebrews for a reason. It's written to people who sacrificed animals for forgiveness at the temple, the Jews (see Hebrews 9:22). Has a Christian ever done this? No we have not. So this passage is not pointed at you, believer.

Yes, this was written to both believers and unbelievers, the author doesn't know who has been saved and who hasn't, but it's specifically directed at Jewish people. The *Hebrews.*

What's the context of Hebrews 10:26? *Repeated animal sacrifices at the temple for sin forgiveness.* These people were used to receiving forgiveness—not by confession or repentance—but only by blood. Along comes Jesus and in essence, says, "You don't have to do that anymore. Just believe I've forgiven you, once, and I will." (Hebrews 1:3, 10:8-9, John 1:29, 8:24, 3:16-18).

After the Good News messengers came through town and told them about Jesus, they had *received knowledge of the truth* but kept on sinning according to the Law of Moses. This required animal blood for atonement, but now, *no animal sacrifice for sins was left.* Jesus dealt with all law-breaking, Mosaic or from the conscience, at the Cross.

Therefore, dear Christian, you don't have to be afraid of Hebrews 10:26 and 27. The individuals who should be afraid are unbelievers who balk at faith in Jesus.

Further, if you keep reading until verse 31, you'll see they trampled on Jesus—on the Spirit of grace—by refusing to turn from the Law and toward faith in Him alone. They had to repent from Moses and believe in Jesus. Are you doing this? No you are not. You have no relationship with Moses' Law and you're fully enjoying God's grace! (See Romans 6:14, Titus 2:11-12, Hebrews 13:9).

With this liberating information we must confront another legalistic elephant in the room: What *will* happen if we deliberately keep on sinning, as Christians.

To answer this, first, how many of our sins are deliberate? All of them. How many of our sins are willful? All of them. We can't accidentally sin, our wills are involved every single time. We're not robots. So if that's the case then what does Hebrews 10:26 mean for us? Nothing. It's not *for* us. We can't apply this to our lives in any way because we're not going to the temple to offer animal sacrifices for sins.

For us, when we sin, God's grace increases. It doesn't decrease or run out but gets bigger. We can't abuse His grace either. That would mean we're wrong when we use it too much, and we always will, unendingly. Paul told the Romans:

> *"The Law was brought in so that the trespass might increase. But where sin increased, grace increased all the more" (Romans 5:20)*

The person who battles legalanity will immediately think I'm saying we should sin. I'm not. *Don't* sin. Sin is bad and not natural to you. Paul faced the same type of people when he wrote to the church in Rome, those who were focused on their "lack" of sinning for righteousness:

> *"What then? Are we to sin because we are not under Law but under grace? By no means!" (Romans 6:15)*

Again, the answer is no. Do not sin. But at the same time, did Paul ever say God's grace would run out *when* they sinned? Never. In fact, he made clear that God's grace *increased.*

More sin, MORE GRACE.

This is hard to fathom for those who are focused on behavior and not identity. Religious thoughts are hard to shake! Many self-proclaimed "devout" individuals cannot get this into their heads: *God has rigged it to where we can't out-sin His grace.* They don't comprehend the power of the blood of Jesus! They think *we*—created finite beings—can somehow offer on *our* part to "make" His blood suffice! Not true, thankfully.

As a result, they revert to Bible passages directed at unbelievers to scare the dickens out of people into *not* sinning. This never works, permanently. Legalists think they need to threaten our forgiveness to make us behave better yet God never does such a thing. He uses grace instead. Only grace can teach us how to live properly, fear cannot (see Titus 2:11-12, 1 John 4:18).

Hebrews 10:26 can be read by believers fearlessly. The one and only sin mentioned in the first ten chapters of Hebrews is unbelief. This is the only unforgivable sin and it's impossible for a Christian to commit it. We've already believed and been reborn, birth is final. We can't be unborn from God's Spirit just the same as we can't be unborn from our mother's womb. Nor can we "walk away" from being born due to poor choices and bad attitudes. It's not possible to "give up" on God. Don't believe that garbage. You can give up on legalism, overbearing church crap, and pressure from religious individuals, but not from your birth into the family of God. He's faithful to you even when you *think* you're faithless (see 2 Timothy 2:13). You cannot lose your salvation and you can't give it up either. You're not more powerful than the blood of Jesus.

These Jewish men and women had received the knowledge of the truth. Who is the truth? Jesus (see John 14:6). They had the best teachers present the news of the gospel yet still wanted to go to the temple to receive forgiveness by animal sacrifices, but no sacrifice for sins was left. Why not? Because Jesus was the last one, on the Cross. He finished all sacrificial requirements for the entire planet (see John 19:30, Hebrews 1:3, 1 John 2:2).

They heard all about Him but said, "Nope. I'm sticking with Moses, animal blood, human priests, and the temple. I'm good. I'm not giving up my tradition for some carpenter's son." They deliberately kept on sinning and had no other way to receive God's forgiveness. Under the Law, without the shedding of animal blood there is no forgiveness. Under grace, without believing in the shed blood of Jesus there is no forgiveness. The Law was now set aside because it's weak and useless, obsolete for all who believe in Messiah. Jesus fulfilled it in Himself! (See Hebrews 3:3-4, 7:18, 8:13, 9:22, Romans 10:4, Galatians 3:24-25).

Christ is now the only way to receive forgiveness from God. His physical body was the final sacrifice:

> *"And by that will we have been sanctified through the offering of the body of Jesus Christ once for all." (Hebrews 10:10)*

> *"For by one offering He has perfected for all time those who are sanctified." (Hebrews 10:14)*

That's you and me, Christian. Therefore *when* we sin, we should turn from it every time but never to receive more forgiveness. Jesus would have to repeatedly die for that to happen (see Hebrews 7:25, 9:26). Instead, we turn from sin to *enjoy* our forgiveness and to *be* our true selves! Holy saints! Children of God! We turn from sin because we've died to it and sin will never make sense in any lasting way! (See Romans 6:2-11, 2 Peter 1:3-9).

So today, my friends, know this: Don't be afraid of Hebrews 10:26. It's not directed at you, believer. *Any* Bible verse which creates fear is not directed at you. You have peace with God (see Romans 5:1,9). You can't mess this up because of the Cross. Due to the Father and Son's promise to one another and *you* becoming the beneficiary to that promise by faith, you're safe (see Hebrews 6:16-19, 9:16-18). God's love is perfect and casts out all fear because fear has to do with punishment (see 1 John 4:18). But Jesus was already punished *plenty* for you. No more sacrifices from Him, or you, is necessary, even when you sin. You are free.

A prayer for you: *Father, thank you for the freedom of biblical context. Since you've taught me to pay close attention to who's being written to and why, all throughout the Bible, it's given me so much confidence in the Cross. How amazing is your grace! Right now, I lift up all who are reading this, directly to you. For some, what they've just read has set them free from fear, but for others, they might want to believe this but are having a hard time. Help them to shift their focus onto the power of Jesus' blood and off sin. The Jews in Hebrews 10:26 refused to do this and that's why they were still your enemies. But for us, we know that Jesus' blood is the most powerful thing ever. We trust it. Amen.*

Day 6

Making an Idol of Making Idols

"Every good and perfect gift is from above"

See James 1:17

"Dad, you're crazy! Why are you like this?!" my daughter blurts out.

"I don't know, Grace, you tell me. You're just *like* me!"

"No, I'm like Mom."

"Nope! You're more of *me* than you are of your mom. The dad is 51% responsible for their child's genetics. The mom is only 49%!"

Whether my statistic is correct or not, Grace shouts, "Darn it! I'm like you!"

We have a good time, Grace and I, roasting one another. Yes, we love each other deeply, we give hugs and affection, saying, "I love you," quite often, but we also enjoy a hearty razz. It's part of our fun-filled, father-daughter relationship. Grace is a blast! I *enjoy* Grace.

One evening, she, Jennifer and I were eating dinner in the living room, cracking up about something, when all of a sudden I got this thought, "You're making an idol of Grace."

What? I said to myself. *Where'd this thought come from?* Since I understand the New Covenant, I instantly knew it wasn't the truth.

I'm enjoying Grace too much? I'm making an idol of her? Ha! Yeah right!

This thought was incorrect, so why did I think it? It could've been the enemy or a representative of his, accusing me (see Revelation 12:10), it could've been the power of sin (see Romans 7:8-11), or it very well could've just been some old stinking thinking (see Romans 12:2). But it happened and I knew it wasn't coming from my spirit or Christ within me.

Ultimately, this idol notion sprang up from some teaching I once sat under as well as a couple books I read which focused on "not making idols in our lives." The Old Testament Commandment of, "Thou shalt not have any other gods before me" was twisted into "no other *idols* before me" which was *then* contorted into: *Anything or anyone in which we get too much pleasure is an idol in our life. Repent quickly and refocus on God as your everything.*

This teaching was, and is, for lack of a better term, dumpster-fire trash. Part of this garbage heaped from pulpits and book pages was, "Pay close attention to what you pay *close* attention to." We had to analyze everything and everyone we derived enjoyment from! A paralysis of analysis ensued as we *had* to be 100% sure we weren't making an idol of anything or anyone, including family members and ourselves! Here are some phrases we heard:

> "Don't make an idol out of your job! It can't save you!"
> "Don't make an idol out of your looks! Stay humble and meek!"
> "You've made an idol out of your own spouse! You've placed them above God and your actions prove that! Repent and put God first!"
> "All you care about is your appearance on social media! Facebook, Snapchat, and Instagram are your idols! Get rid of them, lest you burn!"

Idol this, idol that, idol *them*. Some churches and authors are so focused on *not* making idols it's impossible to enjoy anything let alone *anyone*. Just as soon as we begin to savor a good time or relationship—boom! "Oh no! I'm making an idol out of this!"

This Anno Domini law—which is any "law" we make up on this side of the Cross—has the same effect as any of Moses' 613. For unbelievers, it reveals their need for grace. For believers, it reminds us of the grace we already have.

God's grace allows us to enjoy our hobbies, jobs, sex, relationships, successes, and ourselves. We don't need to focus on *not* having any idols any more than we don't need to focus on *not* shaving the edges of our beards; or for women, *not* thinking, "I'm ceremonially unclean," during that time of the month (see Leviticus 15:19, 19:27).

If we fix our thoughts on protecting ourselves from supposed idols, Satan and the power of sin will have a field day.

Do you like golf? Idol!

Football? Idol!

Netflix? Idol!

Do you like a boyfriend or girlfriend? Idol!

Sports car? Idol!

Weightlifting? Idol!

Grandkids? Idols!

Ministry or talent? Idols!

CrossFit or running? Idol, idol!

Video games? Idol!

Do you enjoy church? Preaching? Volunteering? Missionary work? Idol, idol, idol, idol! Even our struggles can be mistaken as idols. Drug and alcohol abuse? Porn, legalism, and status? Perfectionism, unforgiveness, impatience, and uber-criticism? Our struggles are not idols! They're struggles!

"You worship that idol rather than God!" they'll say. But why do they do this? Simple. It's because they find their own identity in how well they're doing at *not* having idols. It's a fleshy comparison game cloaked from the pulpit, book pages, and internet posts. So what's *their* greatest idol?

Not having any idols.

That's no way to live.

So today, my friends, know this: James said every good and perfect gift is from above! (See James 1:17). God wants us to *enjoy* our lives! He wants us to find great pleasure in our friends, loved ones, occupation, retirement, sports, ministries, leisure, and fruits of our labor! He wants us to wear our blessings well! The good and perfect gifts He's given? Enjoy them! You can even enjoy yourself! God does, why can't you? Making idols of making idols is a silly thing. If you find yourself feeling guilty about taking delight in people, places, and things, do what I did when I thought the same about my own daughter. Enjoy them even more, and thank God, even more.

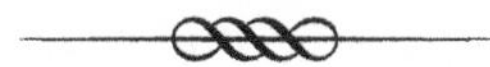

A prayer for you: *Dad, there are times I forget that I'm currently enjoying the very things and people I've prayed for. I asked you for a family, a home, a business, good health, sobriety, and a greater knowledge of your grace. You've given me these wonderful gifts in spades! I'm exceedingly grateful! Right now, I lift up all who are reading this, directly to you. So many of these dear people have faced modern-day idol-worship teaching. Fear, guilt, condemnation, and religious manipulation has caused them so much stress and pain. Some have even forgotten HOW to enjoy their life. They're too afraid of making idols. Let them know that's not possible as your child. You want them to enjoy what you've given them to the fullest, and abundantly. Remind them that you get pleasure from THEM getting pleasure. In Christ's name I pray, amen.*

Day 7

Is Christian Universalism True?

"Today if you hear His voice, do not harden your hearts"

See Hebrews 3:15

The answer to the title of this devotional is, "No, Christian Universalism is not true." If it were, we would have to ignore quite a bit of Scripture about three things:

1. Choosing to believe
2. Evangelism
3. Warnings about hell

What is Christian Universalism? *It's the belief the entire world is saved, whether we like it or not, most just don't realize what Jesus did for everyone. Hell isn't real and nobody will be punished by God.*

This idea began in the early 1800s and continues on today. Christian Universalism gives no one the opportunity to make the *decision* of placing their faith in Jesus, nor can they reject Him. His "universal" love and saving ability *has* saved us. We have no say in the matter. We're safe, secure, and have nothing to worry about in regard to our salvation.

This sounds amazing! But it's just not true, scripturally.

Universalists have a handful of Bible passages they'll use in an attempt to say Jesus' work on the Cross saved *everyone* and fixed the world's sin issue with God. Let's look at a couple:

1. **1 John 2:2** – *"He is the propitiation for our sins, and not for ours only but also for the sins of the whole world."* Propitiation simply means *satisfying sacrifice.* They'll use this passage and point out what I've underlined—"for the sins of the whole world"—which *is* true. Christ's bloody body *did* satisfy the Father's wrath over all sin for all time (see Romans 5:1,9, 6:23, Hebrews 1:3, 10:10,26). The issue is, we must accept this truth by faith *for* our sins. He doesn't force forgiveness onto us. We must receive it by receiving Jesus. Christ is standing at the door of our lives, knocking. We have to make the decision to open up and let Him in by grace through faith. He'll never kick in the door and yell, "Here, take this forgiveness!" Even though He *has* paid for all our sins—past, present, and future—we must still believe, once (see Revelation 3:20, Ephesians 2:8-9, John 3:16-18).
2. **2 Corinthians 5:18-19** – *"Now all these things are from God, who reconciled us to Himself through Christ and gave us the ministry of reconciliation, namely, that God was in Christ reconciling the world to Himself, not counting their trespasses against them, and He has committed to us the word of reconciliation."* This passage from Paul is outstanding! He's explaining what God has done through Jesus, which is reconcile Himself to us! Sadly, the Universalist will pull this passage out of context and say we're *all* reconciled—the

> world—and nobody's sins are counted against them. But we must keep reading through the next verse, "We beg you, be reconciled to God" (see 2 Corinthians 5:20). Why beg if they were already reconciled? Why plead *be reconciled* if Jesus did this without us knowing? Reconciliation takes two willing parties. If I want to reconcile with someone but they refuse, we aren't reconciled. It takes two to tango. *We*—on our part—must believe Christ has saved us from our sins. We must believe God. This is the one-time *saving* faith James talks about, using Abraham and Rahab as examples (see James 2). This is the faith Paul reminded the Galatians of—what's *already* happened—a moment of faith which entered them into a union with our Creator (see Galatians 3).

If Christian Universalism were true, we must also ignore all the Bible passages about evangelism, so get out your Sharpie. Spreading the Good News about Christ wouldn't be necessary because everyone is already saved. So scratch through these verses:

"Today if you hear His voice, do not harden your hearts" (See Hebrews 3:15)

"I am sending you to them to open their eyes and turn them from darkness to light, and from the power of Satan to God, so that they may receive forgiveness of sins and a place among those who are sanctified by faith in me." (See Acts 26:17-18)

"For God so loved the world that He gave His one and only Son, that whoever believes in Him shall not perish but have eternal life. For God did not send His Son into the world to condemn the world, but to

save the world through Him. Whoever believes in Him is not condemned, but whoever does not believe stands condemned already because they have not believed in the name of God's one and only Son."
(John 3:16-18)

And what about this doozy?

"If we confess our sins, He is faithful and just and will forgive us our sins and purify us from all unrighteousness." (1 John 1:9)

Why would a saved person confess something which doesn't exist? We may as well toss out the entire canon of Scripture! We wouldn't need it because we're all good to go!

Wrong. The truth is we have a choice. We can believe or choose to reject faith in Christ. If we're believing God we're believing Christ because Christ *is* God (see John 14:9).

This musters up a logical question we all think at some point or another, so let's just go ahead and tackle it: *What about the people who don't get the opportunity to believe in Jesus because they've never had a chance to hear about Him?*

Why stop there? Let's ask even tougher questions: *What about aborted babies, little children, the handicapped and mentally-impaired?*

Here's my answer: *God is love.*

He *is* love. Love isn't just one of His many characteristics but love is *who* He is (see 1 John 4:8). Therefore we have to trust Him in regard to these topics rather than say all the world is saved because it's not. We mustn't brush these matters off with condescending or appeasing universal answers. We don't need to give the day of the week when someone asks us what time it is. We don't need to be salespeople for God. We can even say,

"I don't know," when we don't know. Our identity isn't found in having all the answers.

I'd advise anyone with difficult thoughts and scenarios to ask God more and more questions. He's a good Father and good fathers never belittle their children's queries. With Him, there's no such thing as a dumb question. He welcomes them all because each question will lead us right back into His great love for humanity.

So what about those who've never had the chance to hear about Jesus? How can they be saved? Here's what I believe the Spirit has taught me: God has presented Himself to everyone on this planet at some point in their lives, and Jesus *is* God.

Friend, there's only one true God. From Creation, He's always made Himself known to each and every person who's ever lived, both before and after the Cross. Paul informs the Romans:

> *"For since the creation of the world God's invisible qualities—His eternal power and divine nature—have been clearly seen, being understood from what has been made, so that people are without excuse." (Romans 1:20)*

There's no mention of Jesus because no chance to believe in Him had been given, yet God is *clearly* seen. Keep in mind, this is Romans 1. The first five chapters of this letter is Paul building his case for *all* of humanity's problem *apart* from God, both the Jews and non-Jews, we Gentiles.

For us, Gentiles, we're without excuse and must believe Him when He presents Himself *through* His creation. What we're seeing around us *causes* us to naturally think, "Where did all this come from?"

This continues today, even with the smartest scientists, because even they will tell you something can't come from nothing. Matter cannot create itself. Something *has* to come from something *else* which always *has been* and always *will be*. That's the God of the Bible. That's Christ; the Word; the Lamb. No beginning or end. The First and the Last. Alpha and Omega. God is timeless! This is why He calls Himself, "I Am!" (See Exodus 3:14, John 1:1,29, 8:58, Revelation 22:13).

Atheistic scientists have a serious origin problem and they know it. Ultimately this is where their arguments dissolve. With no other way to defend their theory, personal attacks and insults become their only defense. When "reason" can't come up with a Creator, because they know *something* created us, they'll get furious or laugh. It's really sad. Why not just say, "*A* god made this."? But they won't. Pride prevents it. If they concede to a god of creation then they must figure out which one is the truth. It's Jesus (see John 14:6).

Some of the most intelligent people claim a Big Bang happened but even *they* will tell you they don't know what caused the bang. I do. It was God when He said, "Let there be light!" (See Genesis 1:3).

Whereas we Gentiles look up at the sky and "believing a god is real" is at least an option set into motion, for the Jews, they must believe in Him *apart* from the Law (see Romans chapters 2-4). After all, they already know where the sun, moon, stars, and humans came from. Moses wrote about it in Genesis after God told him.

The Jews weren't special, per se. Yes, the Word chose their race to become physical flesh; and yes, they got to carry the oracles of human history. But even they had to believe God at some point. That is, each, individual person. Being a Jew by birth did not make them right with God. The righteous have always lived by faith, through simply believing God. The Law never made anyone righteous. It simply increased one's awareness of a deep need for a graceful Savior (see Romans 1:17, 5:20, 10:4, Galatians 3:11).

Solomon, a Jew, even he said God has written the notion of eternity in the heart of every human, not just the Hebrews (see Ecclesiastes 3:11). Believing the One True God is what saves a person. Seek and you will find. Knock and the door will be opened. "Why am I here, God? Who are you?" Every human can ask these questions and He'll always answer.

"In past generations He allowed all the nations to walk in their own ways. Yet He did not leave Himself without witness" (See Acts 14:16-17)

Since the beginning of time, faith has always been the way into a relationship with God, even for Gentiles. This is why Paul said *all* the nations. Before the Cross, believing God—faith—*credited* accounts because Christ's blood payment goes forward *and* backwards. He's not bound by time, we are. He created the planets—their rotations and revolutions—and the sun in which we get our notion of time *from* (see 2 Peter 3:8, Revelation 13:8). So if we can be saved by faith thousands of years after the Cross, why can't others be saved by faith thousands of years before it? The answer is, they can!

I go deeper into this subject in a devotional titled, *Jesus Has Retroactive Blood,* from, *The Christian Identity, Volume 2.*

Before the Cross, God left all sins committed by the believing Jew *and* the believing Gentile unpunished until the moment Christ died.

"For there is no distinction: for all have sinned and fall short of the glory of God, and are justified by His grace as a gift, through the redemption that is in Christ Jesus, whom God put forward as a propitiation by His blood, to be received by faith. This was to show God's righteousness, because in His divine forbearance he had passed over former sins." (See Romans 3:22-25)

Forbearance? That means He was patient. He was patiently waiting for the Cross to happen as believers sinned all the time with *no* distinction in their race. And do you see what I underlined? The sins before Christ's death were passed over, but not just for the Jews! Again, there was no distinction! This included my heathen forefathers who believed God, and yours too, Gentile! Another translation reads, "He had left the sins committed beforehand unpunished." How were sins unpunished before the Cross happened?

Credited righteousness by faith.

By believing God. Abraham lived way before Jesus did and Paul used him as an example of credited righteousness:

> *What does Scripture say? "Abraham believed God, and it was credited to him as righteousness." (Romans 4:3, {Paul quoting Genesis 15:6})*

Someone might say, "Well Abraham was a Jew, that's why he received a righteousness credit put on his books"—but hold on. Rahab was *not* a Jew, she lived *before* the Cross, and she too was credited as righteous by faith—by simply *believing* God (see James 2:25, Hebrews 11:31).

This proves God has always been interested in one main thing, "Do you believe me?" If you do, once, you are right with Him forever. From the time of Adam and Eve that's all He's ever wanted. Had they believed Him—that they were *already* perfect—they wouldn't have eaten from the tree to receive the devil's legalistic knowledge of right and wrong.

Lastly, what about hell? Universalists say a loving God would never send someone to such a torturous place. They claim it doesn't even exist. However, Jesus spoke more about hell than He did heaven. There are warnings all throughout Scripture. Hell is real and hell is bad. It's specifically reserved for those who reject God—His enemies. I'm no expert on hell because my focus is on how *not* to go there: *Faith in Jesus Christ.*

But I do know this, God is not *sending* people to hell. It's them *choosing* unbelief over believing Him. Whereas heaven is the complete absence of sin, hell is the most potent place of it. There's no hope there.

I used to think hell never ended because there's scriptures which indicate it doesn't end. But an argument has surfaced lately which I've heard from trusted colleagues. It's the *thought*—not the proof—that God will ultimately *destroy* hell and all who are there, annihilation. The word *destruction* is the basis. Yet, I don't know. Why take the chance, unbeliever?

Whether it ends or not, hell is explicitly booked for the enemies of God, the devil, and his demons (see Matthew 25:41). Do not go there. You decide, God doesn't. Believe Him right now if you haven't. If you have, don't worry about hell. You're already seated in heaven, spiritually (see Ephesians 2:6).

Do babies, children, and handicapped people who obviously have the mind of children, go to hell? I don't see that in Scripture. I see Jesus saying the kingdom of God belongs to such as these (see Matthew 19:14, Mark 10:14, Luke 18:16). When David's baby died, he said, "I will go to be with him one day" (see 2 Samuel 12:23).

I think I'll trust that. I think I'll trust the love of God.

So today, my friends, know this: The whole world isn't saved. We must believe God. If you're on a remote island and have never heard about Jesus, God is still there because God is Jesus. His Holy Spirit is wooing you through your conscience and creation. That palm tree? He made that. Those seagulls and vast ocean? He dreamt that up. Believe Him today! The message about Christ must continue to spread because countless people have rejected God's Spirit by faith. This message *must* continue until His return so we can all be built up into the full knowledge of His great love!

A prayer for you: *God—Father, Son, Holy Spirit—thank you for life. Thank you for creating us. Even though we descended from our sinful*

forefather, Adam, therefore inheriting sin by no fault of our own, you made a way for us to become righteous by faith in Christ—by no works of our own. Thank you for making a way before the world began! Right now, I lift up all who are reading this, directly to you. For the believer, take them deeper into the truths of your grace. Reveal just how loving you are and how much you care for the entire world. For the unbeliever, keep calling them, Lord. Keep reminding them you're there with arms wide open, whenever they want to turn to you. Amen.

Day 8

When Kobe Died

"You do not even know what will happen tomorrow. What is your life? You are a mist that appears for a little while and then vanishes."

James 4:14

"Dad! It's Mom!" Grace yells with eyes wide open, stretching out her clutched phone while sitting on the bleachers.

"What." I reply, not asking a question, but letting her know I didn't want to talk. We just finished a game and I wanted to wipe off with a towel and get a drink from the water fountain.

"Kobe died!" Grace shouts.

"Are you serious?" I take the phone and put it up to my ear.

"Matt, Kobe Bryant just died in a helicopter crash."

"You're joking," I pause, waiting for her to say, "Gotcha!"

"I'm not joking at all! He's dead!" Jennifer replies.

After saying, "Oh my goodness, that's terrible," I look at Grace and slowly hand her back the phone. Shocked, thinking, *This ain't real. It's gotta be a gag,* I step back down the bleachers and head onto the court. The other eight men were waiting for Grace and me to start the next game.

"Kobe just died," I informed them. They all paused and slowly turned toward me, one by one. I continue, "Yeah, in a helicopter crash."

"Oh my gosh."

"No..."

"He was my favorite player."

"You gotta be kidding me!"

Each man had something to say, Grace then joined us and we played the next game, sorta in a haze. It was weird, and it was definitely my last game for the day.

Every Sunday afternoon Grace and I go to the Civic Center to practice and then run full court with other grown men for a couple hours. But this day was like 9/11, seared into my memory forever.

I could tell the news of Kobe's death really hit Grace hard, especially when we were leaving the gym. We found out Gigi died too, one of his daughters, along with several others.

Grace and I have a relationship like Kobe and Gianna in the fact that we bond over basketball. She and I both follow Kobe and Gigi's activity on Instagram, along with Vanessa, Kobe's wife. They're always sharing videos of Gianna playing ball, and Kobe goes to all these different games with her, sitting sideline and enjoying daddy-daughter time. It warmed my heart to see these occasions they spent together, especially because of Gigi being close to the same age as Grace.

So after stopping to get a shake, Grace and I rode home. I tried to talk to her about the tragedy because I could see her mind was racing. It was really sad to see Grace sad. When we got home she went to her room and Jennifer and I watched NBA TV for the rest of the night in dismay and sorrow. It wasn't just my wife and I who were in shock, it looked like the whole world.

I normally post a few times a day on my social media pages, but I couldn't pull myself to do it. Facebook and Instagram had become memorials and there was no way to not see how terrible this day was.

I used to hate Kobe Bryant, not as a person, but as a basketball player—and not *hate* as in "I wished him harm"—but his Lakers were *so* unstoppable. Nobody was even close. That bothered me because I didn't live in L.A., I grew up watching MJ and the Bulls, and here comes this cocky teenager who mimicked every single move of Michael Jordan's down to the way he chewed his gum. He was just so darned talented! Talented like Mike! We all wanted to be like Mike from the first time that Gatorade jingle was played, but Kobe actually did it! And we were jealous! The whole league was too!

I've been an NBA fanatic since the sixth grade, 1992. I got a poster of Michael Jordan from Walmart when I was in a Boys Home in Palatka, Florida. I hung it up next to my bed and would stare at it for what seemed like hours. He was in the sky with clouds around him, and Michael was floating...

Gazing at MJ in my room while laying on my bed, when I was normally in trouble, I became infatuated with everything Jordan. I daydreamed about how good he was and the things he did on the court. Michael Jordan was an escape for me while I was in the custody of the State. For a time, Mom and Dad both lost guardianship of us kids. We were all split up, and in pain. At that young age a month seemed like a decade and my soul hurt most of the time. Misbehaving was how I coped. I was furious, heartbroken, I didn't like the other boys, and I felt all alone.

After discovering MJ's superpowers, I got every book I could find on him from the library. When the *Scholastic Book Fairs* would come to town, I'd beg for some money to get the latest Chicago Bulls books. I collected all things

Michael. Cards, newspaper clippings, figurines, cereal boxes, anything. He was the escape from my reality of being the foster kid from the Boys Ranch.

And then Kobe happened in 1996. I already knew about Kobe Bryant because I had the *USA Today* of the top high school players from that year; a picture of him was in it. I also watched the press conference where he declared his eligibility for the NBA, therefore bypassing college. I had *also* seen SportsCenter footage of him massacring his high school competition. He was nothing like other NBA players and he'd not yet played a single NBA minute—and, he was only 17.

What made him so special was nobody had *ever* emulated Michael Jordan with such intricate detail. Now *this* is what bothered me so much about him. The footwork, the fade-away, the killer instinct, the way he attacked the basket with all ferocity. He *was* Mike—reincarnated it seemed! To make matters "worse" the most dominant center of all time, Shaq, joined him!

"Not fair!"

I was a Laker hater in the fullest. I'm not gonna lie. I couldn't *stand* how good they were! I wanted Reggie to get a ring! I wanted AI to get one too! And Mutombo! Mark Jackson! I loved the Fab Five and Kobe robbed Jalen of a championship *and* he dropped 81 on him! How disrespectful!

"Nobody can stop Kobe and Shaq but Kobe copied Michael and can't win without Shaq!"

I was a member of Laker Hater Anonymous, but I wasn't anonymous about it. I couldn't stand seeing them on all the magazines and I *really* couldn't stand Rick Fox with his lush, curly hair and Hollywood grin. But the truth was, I couldn't stand how dominant they were.

When the Pistons finally beat them in the Finals and that team dissolved, I was ecstatic! I know I wasn't alone. When you see a team *so* good and win *so* much, and they aren't your team, saltiness is typically your flavor of choice. I wouldn't admit it back then, but I'd take that team, the Lakers from the early 2000s, over the 95-96 Bulls. Kobe *and* Shaq? Forget about it. Greatest duo of all time.

Like Mike and Scottie did to so many NBA teams in the 1990s, Shaq and Kobe did the following decade. Charles, Pat, Karl, and John, they would've all gotten their rings but Mike was too great. Same with Kobe and Shaq; and then Kobe did it *again, twice* without the big man, proving his supremacy in the game and elite status.

The older I got—and the older Kobe became as well—I started to like him, a lot. Whereas he seemed to be an assassin with no regard for human life on the court, off the court, he was genuine, friendly, funny, and inspirational. Recently I learned *on* the court he was kind as well. Even Jalen Rose said, "When he scored 81 on me, he never trashed talked one time. He was respectful and just went about his business."

The interviews, the time he spent teaching younger players, and the joy he expressed, I became a Kobe fan. No longer was I disliking him but appreciating him as a person.

He was unstoppable, even a busted Achilles couldn't hold him down. Kobe Bean Bryant was poetry in motion, and graceful—not like Mike but like *himself*. For 20 years I got to witness this fascinating player whom I had animosity toward because he was marvelous, like my childhood hero. I wouldn't say this in the barbershop as Luke cut my hair, but after his last game in 2016, going out with 60 points and then thanking Vanessa for holding down the fort all those years—I loved Kobe.

Kobe was a top three basketball player who ever lived. Arguably the best.

However, more than anything else—more than any breathtaking highlight I ever saw of Kobe's—the most amazing sight I witnessed?…Watching him with his family on Instagram. The way he doted on his wife and children was the most poignant, meaningful thing I ever saw from him. No iconic basketball moment compares. Whereas so many professional athletes fall off the deep end after retirement—or do so during their career and are forced *into* retirement—Kobe *loved* his family, even to the end. The glow on his face when he played with his girls or spent time with his wife was greater than the glow he had while receiving *any* of his five rings.

What was he doing during his last moments on earth? Taking his little girl to go play basketball. That's what Grace and I do...

I can't imagine the helplessness he felt as he knew the helicopter was going down, clutching Gigi I'm sure. I can't imagine the Altobelli's, the Chester's, Christina Mauser, and Ara Zobayan—the instant panic they faced... and I don't want to. If anything positive could come of this crash, it's that they didn't suffer. It was an instant death for them all. I've seen the footage and there's no way they felt a thing.

So today, my friends, know this: Life on earth is but a vapor. We don't get to take anything with us to our next life except for people, so express Jesus when you get the chance. With all of Kobe's accomplishments on the basketball court, being a loving leader for his family was his life's pinnacle. He had just taken Gigi to church that morning and he *was* a believer. In an interview with Stephen A. Smith in the mid-2000s, after his rape charge and family problems, he told Stephen A., "God is good." Kobe also said he let Jesus carry his cross for him. Now *this* is what saves. That is, letting Christ do what we can't, by grace through faith. We Christians will all see Kobe and Gigi again.

A prayer for Vanessa, the Bryant girls, and the families of the victims: *Heavenly Father, right now, I lift up these dear people directly to you. The pain they're feeling, I cannot even understand, but you can. You feel their agony, I know you do. Jesus showed us this. Today, I ask for you*

to let them know you're there. I ask for you to comfort them on the deepest level possible. Remind them of your great love and the promise of reuniting with their loved ones in the future. Through faith in Christ we'll all meet again one sweet day. No more death. No more mourning. No more tears or pain. Strengthen them with your grace. It is sufficient for all our needs. Amen.

Day 9

He Must Increase, I Must Decrease?

"But now He has reconciled you by Christ's physical body through death to present you holy, unblemished, and blameless in His presence"

Colossians 1:22

I normally will build up to my point in each devotional, but let's just get right to it:

GOD DOES NOT EXPECT CHRISTIANS TO DECREASE SO CHRIST CAN INCREASE.

I'd love to put an exclamation point at the end of that statement, but I'll leave it as it is. When John the Baptist said, "He must increase, I must decrease," he was *not* talking about himself as a person (see John 3:30). He was *not* trying to appear humble to look good in front of a congregation. He was *not* exuding false humility "so that" he could point to Jesus.

HE WAS TALKING ABOUT THE MOSAIC LAW.

John the Baptist preached Moses not Jesus. He taught Israel to repent back *toward* obeying Moses not *toward* obeying Jesus. How can I say that? Because the Old Covenant was still in full force because the Cross had not yet happened. Each time he yelled, "Repent!" he longed for a Messiah to come along and put an end to his legalistic ministry of teaching 613 commandments given by Moses to *only* the Israelites. We are Gentiles, we were not included. But then again, even if you're reading this as a Jew, you still have to turn to Jesus and away from Moses (see Hebrews 3:3-12, 10:26-29).

John wasn't attempting to get the approval of those following him by appearing meek. He was expressing the need for grace and truth, the need for Jesus.

"For the Law was given through Moses; grace and truth came through Jesus Christ." (John 1:17)

There's not much good news in the four gospels. Sure, there's some, but it's mostly Mosaic Law being taught in order to get self-righteous people to see they were absolute failures at obeying it. Why? So they would repent *from* the Law and *toward* grace; toward faith in the One who would save them from their Mosaic infractions (see James 2:10, Galatians 3:10). Now *this* is what would decrease, Law teaching, not John. Not me or you, dear Christian.

Law *observance*—not Law itself—would soon fade away. Once Christ went to the Cross it would become obsolete for all who would believe in the Son of God (see Matthew 5:18, Hebrews 8:12-13, Romans 6:14, 10:4).

John was talking about—LAW. LAW. LAW. LAW. LAAAAAAAAAAW.

Not you.

So when someone tries to use the passage of "I must decrease, He must increase" as a *Christian* to *prove* their humbleness, they just don't understand what actually happened to them the moment of their salvation—NEWNESS.

"Therefore, if anyone is in Christ, he is a new creation. The old has passed away; behold, the new has come." (2 Corinthians 5:17)

"But now He has reconciled you by Christ's physical body through death to present you holy, unblemished, and blameless in His presence" (Colossians 1:22)

"In Christ you have been brought to fullness." (See Colossians 2:10)

Are we just going to ignore these passages to appear modest? Are we going to say the Cross didn't fully work so *we* still need to decrease? Why not just take God for His word and believe what He says about us? Why not just believe what Jesus did *to* us not just *for* us? Is it because we still sin and make mistakes? If that's what you think dear believer, let me tell you something:

YOU ARE NOT YOUR MISTAKES.

You are not your accomplishments. You are not your mundane actions and attitudes. You are a spotless, holy, blameless, new creation, child of God, set apart, currently-seated-in-heaven RIGHTEOUS SAINT. Separate your *who* from your *do* to understand this. We don't need to mix the Covenants or twist John the Baptist's words. Just be yourself! Yeah, I said that! Be you!

Before salvation should we decrease? Even to that I'd say no. The Pharisees sure thought such a thing; that way they could put on a show of humility. But not you, Christian. It was the *Law* which needed to decrease so that *grace* could come in! For us? We don't decrease—we died! Our spirits were literally crucified with Christ! Dead, not decreased! Buried, not decreased! Raised back to life as new! NOT DECREASED! (See Romans 6:6-10, Galatians 2:20, 2 Corinthians 5:21).

You should *increase*! Learn! Grow! Mature! Don't *decrease* as a Christian but flourish and have your mind renewed! Walk *out* who you *are*! Increase, increase, increeeeeeeeease! (See Galatians 5:22-23, 2 Peter 3:18).

"But Matt, I need to give God all the glory!"

Friend, He already had all the glory. Why do you think He remade you and then connected Himself *to* you? He wants to live *through* you! Jesus said He has now given *you* all the glory! (See John 17:22).

"Matt, that seems so conceited!"

But it's not! It's called confidence in what God has done to you! It's what *Jesus* wants! He didn't recreate you so you could lie about yourself! He wants you to express Him! This is *how* you will exude the glory of God within you!

I'll tell you what's conceited, ignoring what God has done to you in order to earn the approval of legalists and quasi-grace teachers who are never proud of you. What's conceited is retrofitting John the Baptist and Moses into what the Cross has accomplished for all who have believed.

"But I gotta make disciples of disciples! We have to produce!"

Do you? What would happen if you didn't? Punishment? No. Jesus was already punished plenty. I'll tell you what would happen: THE ROCKS WOULD CRY OUT, "JESUS IS LORD! BELIEVE!" (See Luke 19:39-40). God would still find a way—BECAUSE HE IS GOD! The salvation of the world is His responsibility not ours! Who do we think we are?! We are not God!...We are His children. His creations.

Why not just *be* and *rest* and let God do what He wants *through* us? "Gotta" make disciples and "gotta" produce? That seems like a lot of pressure to me, yet a vine *never* pressures a branch to produce, which is what our relationship is with the Spirit of Christ (see John 15:5, Galatians 5:22-23).

Further, that word *disciple* isn't mentioned in any letter to any church in the New Testament, not once. Don't you think if making disciples of disciples was so crucial, Paul, Peter, Jude, John, James—they would've told the ecclesia about it at least one time? But they didn't. In the book of Acts, which was *recorded acts* not doctrine—which means the body of Christ was getting things in order and purging immature theology—this was the last time *disciples* was used.

Disciples simply describes followers who learn. Once the early Christians realized we have something much better than following—that we are *in*—that word wasn't used by any group of believers again (see Hebrews 3:6, Colossians 3:3, 1 Corinthians 6:17). If a person *must* harp on that term, I think the best way, for them, is to *not* look at making disciples as an individual goal, but as a corporate thing for the entire body of believers.

We can be disciples of Dora the Explorer if we wanted. David Koresh had disciples, so did John the Baptist. Even Jesus did before Pentecost. WE NOW HAVE SOMETHING SUPERIOR! AN EVENT WHICH HAPPENED IN ACTS 2! THE SPIRIT IN US AND US IN HIM!

God is inside of you, Christian. You are inside of Him. Like cereal in milk and milk in cereal. Separate yet one. The milk is not following the cereal and the cereal is not following the milk. You are *one.*

"But whoever is united with the Lord is one with Him in spirit."
(1 Corinthians 6:17)

We are learning from within not following someone. We are new creations who *have* the Spirit of God. We are called to *live* and *be* and express our Creator with ease. He does the rest as we rest in Him. He's who woos and calls and molds. We are the branches, not the vine. Branches grow without stress or strain, depending on the vine for everything; and the vine definitely isn't telling the branches to decrease! He wants us to grow, organically!

It pains me to hear Christians told they need to decrease so Jesus can increase. The truth is, we each have all we need for life and godliness (see 2 Peter 2:13). The only thing that should decrease is our old actions and attitudes which don't match up with who we now are. Even better, it is God who causes this growth over the course of our lifetime, not us (see Philippians 1:6, 2:13, Colossians 2:19).

God isn't expecting us to lie about ourselves so that uber-critical people, religious relatives, and Law teachers can say, "Oh look at them. How modest. How meek. God is so proud of their humility."

Blah!

Be you. If your personality is loud and boisterous, be you. If it's quiet and you enjoy a more low-key atmosphere, be you. You *need* to be you, Christian. Life will never make sense until you begin expressing your true self. Don't fall for the lie that false humility is the way to go, and don't you *ever* talk bad about yourself. The Spirit within you will counsel you when you get off track, but make no mistake, He's never guiding you to be less of you. He's renewing your mind to your absolute righteousness instead. He's teaching you how to live moment by moment, gently and patiently, both with yourself and others.

So today, my friends, know this: If you've placed your faith in Jesus, increase in who you are. Be *being* filled. Don't decrease. If you haven't, today is your day of death and resurrection, not simply decreasing. Believe Christ has saved you from your sins and He will. Unbelievers don't need to be less of themselves so Jesus can be more in them. He won't even join them until they're new. But once He does, He does so permanently because we've been made perfect in our identity by one offering, His body on the Cross.

Perfection doesn't need to decrease. Therefore increase, and grow (see Hebrews 10:10,14, Philippians 4:13).

A prayer for you: *Father, thank you for my new identity. You gave me this identity as a young boy, when I first believed, but because of two-timing teaching I didn't understand it. For so long I thought I had to keep decreasing, but that's a big fat lie. I needed to increase, mature, and grow. Keep teaching me more about this truth. Right now, I lift up all who are reading this, directly to you. I'm sad for those who've been beat down by Mosaic legalism. Just because someone on stage tells them they need to decrease so Jesus can increase, they put on a show of self-abasement. They talk bad about themselves to appear humble. Dad, please take them deeper into the knowledge of what you've done to them as your child. Help them to discern the Old Covenant of Law from the New Covenant of grace—of Jesus. Help them to be able to point out the false teachings about their identity as your kids. Even when they hear hypnotizing music in church, such as "More of you… and less of me… take ev… ry… thing…" As a believer, this does not apply to them. It's not, "More of you and less of me," it's both of us. It's a beautiful relationship. We thank you for this. In Christ's name, amen.*

Day 10

The Truth About Demon-Casting and Fasting

"Let us hold fast the confession of our hope without wavering, for he who promised is faithful."

Hebrews 10:23

Early one morning, in the Fall of 2019, I woke up and checked my messages as I normally do. With eyes still squinting, waiting on my coffee to brew, one email in particular stood out to me:

"Matt, I've been serving God since 1979. A good friend of mine who wasn't a Christian came to stay in my home. I witnessed her being attacked by demons. Me, being a Christian, I told her about Jesus and she became one too. However, the demonic attacks went on for years, even when she moved to her own apartment. Satan has no shame in attacking God's children, he even continued to lure her into the church's basement, caressing her, and

leaving marks. Years went by and eventually she was only set free through prayer and fasting. God is faithful."

Now, before I understood the New Covenant, I would've simply read this, replied "Amen," and then moved on with my day. However, there's glaring inconsistencies of what Scripture teaches us based on the covenant Christ brought in at Calvary.

1. **Satan cannot *touch* a Christian, physically.** The only power he has against children of God is accusations; demons, the same. Scripture is clear, "The evil one cannot touch you," John tells us this truth (see 1 John 5:18). In Revelation, he also reveals the devil's only weapon, "The accuser of our brothers and sisters accuses them day and night" (see Revelation 12:10). Accusations. Accusations. Accusations. That's it. He's a liar who lies like a fish that swims. *When* he lies he's speaking in his native tongue (see John 8:44). His dark idiots who do his bidding copy him. He lies to us about who we are, about others, about our future, our past; he lies about absolutely anything we can think of which causes stress, pain, factions, and inadequacy. But, he has no right to *touch* us—only unbelievers.
2. **Satan cannot *touch* a Christian, spiritually.** I was watching a documentary some years back about a church with a pastor who "specialized" in casting out demons (heavy on the quotation marks). His congregation couldn't go without a weekly or monthly exorcism. The focus wasn't on Jesus but on a charade; demons "arguing" with this man, patrons flailing on the floor and screaming. Then they'd barf the unclean spirit out and sleep for a while, kept warm by a holy blanket. Where is this in any New Testament epistle? Nowhere, from Romans to Revelation. Acts is not an epistle but a book of the recorded *acts* of

the early, immature church. We'll get to that shortly. Unfortunately, for the people whom the pastor just exorcised their demon, it would come back the next day, or Wednesday, or whenever. "I'll just have to go see Pastor on Sunday to get rid of it again," they told the person interviewing them. Friend, it's *impossible* for a Christian to be possessed by a demon because we're literally possessed by the Holy Spirit of Jesus Christ (see 1 Corinthians 6:17,19). He's not sharing your spirit nor body with anything from hell. In fact, the instant you believed, He sealed you up forever *with* Him (see Ephesians 1:13, Colossians 3:3). Only unbelievers can be possessed by demons, not Christians. God won't allow it. Yes, we can be *o*ppressed, as in, they can pester us with accusations and scare tactics—especially if we give them lots of attention—but never can a demon enter us. *Jesus* lives in us, permanently. He'd whoop them if they tried. So *stomp* at their dumb butts like the barking dogs they are. Paul did this to a demon-possessed female in Acts 16, but only after she wouldn't stop annoying him for days. And there wasn't a ritual, he simply said, "Back off!" So mostly, pay them no mind and focus on Christ and who *you* are.

3. **Fasting does not cast out demons, nor does it change God's mind.** Prayer changes things, yes, mainly our perspective, but fasting does not.

Before I continue with fasting, I want you to know God is paying close attention to you, dear Christian. Not so much your efforts, not so much your works, but you. You're His child and He cares about you *so* much. If you're in a habit of fasting and you want to do that, then do that. But please know that God isn't sitting back with His hands folded until you start or stop any particular *thing*. He's a good Father, and good fathers don't work that way. He loves you, and fasting isn't increasing His love nor causing Him to move.

In Mark 9:29, there's a passage about Jesus casting out a demon. He said such can only be done by prayer and fasting. However, earlier transcripts have been found since this was originally allowed in the canon of Scripture. Earlier transcripts means more accurate text and the word *fasting* isn't there. What does this mean? Likely a scribe wrote it incorrectly. It's been removed since this discovery in many versions of the Bible. The same goes for Mark 16:9-20, which includes these two verses:

> *"And these signs will accompany those who believe: in my name they will cast out demons; they will speak in new tongues; they will pick up serpents with their hands; and if they drink any deadly poison, it will not hurt them; they will lay their hands on the sick, and they will recover."* (Mark 16:17-18)

This block of text is gone, now that older transcripts of the original manuscripts have been unearthed. What does this tell us? *The basis of fasting to cast out demons isn't biblical and making deadly choices isn't smart.*

Yes, tongues is mentioned in the epistles, which is foreign language speaking; a sign to the unbeliever by hearing the gospel in their native tongue (see 1 Corinthians 14:22). Praying for others to recover from sickness is too (see James 5:14-15). But we must listen to the Spirit's guidance in all things *then* look to Scripture to back Him up—not the other way around.

I understand this might hurt the egos of the demon-casters, but such is a good thing! If that's you, friend, just think about the pressure which has now been taken off you and placed onto Jesus. You don't *have* to perform exorcisms any longer. You are free!

If you still don't believe me, do your own research and I trust you'll uncover the same. Our job, as Christians, is not to constantly cast out demons but to preach Jesus (see 1 Corinthians 1:23, 2:2). Don't you think if demon-casting is to be our main objective we would've received instructions in at least one epistle? Yet it's not there—nor is fasting for that matter. Fasting can have physical health benefits but not *spiritual* health benefits.

These letters are void of a single directive about either topic, all were written subsequent to the Cross and maturity of the apostles:

Romans, 1 Corinthians, 2 Corinthians, Galatians, Ephesians, Philippians, Colossians, 1 Thessalonians, 2 Thessalonians, 1 Timothy, 2 Timothy, Titus, Philemon, Hebrews, James, 1 Peter, 2 Peter, 1 John, 2 John, 3 John, Jude, Revelation

Not one lesson or edification to fight demons or fast. In the four gospels? Yes, but fasting in Matthew, Mark, Luke, and John was never a command for believers. On the contrary, Christ scolds unbelieving legalists who wanted to be praised for their fasting (see Matthew 6:16-18). This proves fasting was a matter of the Law as those Jews found their "righteousness" in obeying Moses' commandments not Jesus'. Christians aren't under the Law but under grace:

"For sin shall no longer be your master, because you are not under the Law, but under grace." (Romans 6:14)

Some disciples of John the Baptist asked why *Jesus'* disciples didn't fast. The answer was because Christ was still with them and their focus was to be on *Him* and nothing else (see Mark 2:18-20). This teaches us the true meaning of fasting which is *focusing on God alone.*

Fasting was never meant to trade off anguish for favor with our Creator. He's not a vindictive sadist. Fasting doesn't accomplish *anything* in the supernatural realm. The reality is, God needs nothing from us. He's God. Even deeper, His ultimate desire is to give *us* life, breath, and everything else! (See Acts 17:25).

What about fasting the book of Acts? It's mentioned twice (see Acts 13:2, 14:23). What we must keep in mind is that Acts isn't a book of doctrine but of recorded *acts* of the apostles. It's a history book of the early, green church; documentation of their unripe actions as the truth began to spread. This is *not* a letter from an apostle to a church or person for holy direction or firm rebuke. In Acts, everyone was getting their belief of Christ alone in order. We're reading chronicles of those events. Therefore we cannot use this book to build a theology in the same way we can't use any history book to build a theology.

Think about it, if we're going to look to Acts as doctrine then we must circumcise people. Why? Because Paul did this to Timothy (see Acts 16:1-5). He obviously outgrew this immature Law-tradition thinking because Paul was livid with the Galatians for allowing circumcision to sneak into their church (see Galatians 5:2).

Further, if Acts sets the standard for church planting then we must all speak a foreign language and have a flame above our heads when we're saved (see Acts 2:1-8). However, Paul informed the Corinthians, "Not everyone speaks in tongues, do they?" (See 1 Corinthians 12:30).

What about Ananias and Sapphira? They dropped dead because they lied about money (see Acts 5:1-11). If this were doctrine our churches would be littered with corpses every time the offering plate is passed around. And were they saved? It doesn't say. And did God kill them? Well does He kill people for lying about money? Earth's population would drop drastically if this were doctrine. There's not enough information about this event to make a conclusion based on the facts of the gospel. Luke simply reveals they lied about money and died after they got caught.

Do you see it, friend? Acts isn't doctrine. Sure, we can glean from it, but we have tons of doctrine *after* this book; after maturity in Christ came to life in the minds, actions, and attitudes of countless Christians. We're all learning and growing, the early church did too.

Accordingly, fasting isn't doctrine for Christians. If you want to fast, fast. That's your prerogative and you're free. But if you're believing you'll have a "banner year" because you're starving yourself, friend, no. God is better to you than that. He doesn't answer your prayers in a greater way because you're hungry. If that were the case then each time we have a need let's just not eat until our situation changes. Eat. It might give you a healthier viewpoint because your blood sugar isn't low, therefore impacting your brain.

So today, my friends, know this: Ignore the demons, eat a sandwich, and focus on Jesus. If you're having a problem with demons, you'll be surprised at how they go away when you pay them no mind. As for fasting from food, social media, sex, sugar—whatever—God doesn't change His mind because you're giving stuff up temporarily. He loves you and doesn't barter His love by way of abstaining from what you enjoy. Instead, it's God who showed His love for *you* by giving up His Son.

A prayer for you: *Heavenly Father, the Bible instructs us to hold fast rather than to fast food, according to the New Covenant. Our hope in Jesus is what we're truly holding fast to. No apostle informs us to fast in order to achieve anything with you, or to appear more holy than others, or to entertain demons. Thank you for this freedom in your Word. Right now, I lift up all who are reading this, directly to you. Help them to understand*

that even before the Cross, fasting was all about focusing on you by giving up food for a time. Food, festivals, and gatherings were Israel's primary method of fun and entertainment. They were instructed to give this up so they can concentrate on your greatness—but you turned the tables! You revealed what YOU gave up! Actually WHO you gave up—Jesus! Help us to focus on Him like you have. Amen.

Day 11

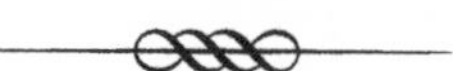

Addiction Recovery Is Not My Identity

"See what great love the Father has lavished on us, that we should be called children of God! And that is what we are!"

See 1 John 3:1

My addiction recovery used to be my identity, or so I thought. My ministry was centered around it, the things I wrote in my books and posted on social media; all my efforts were pointed toward, "Let me show you what you need to do to quit."

Sure, I helped some people, but there was a much better way which would germinate into the souls of others and create stronger roots of sobriety. I needed to cut the string of the dangling carrot:

"Give it all you've got! Don't give up!
Discipline yourself and you'll achieve your goal!"

Whereas straining might work at first, white-knuckling is based on *trying* and not trusting. I needed to teach people to trust God, not try harder. We are branches and He is the vine (see John 15:5). Branches never try to do anything. They simply *live* while depending on their source of life. They rest and just *be*. I needed to mature into resting in who I am.

To make matters worse, because of learned legalism, in May of 2014—when I first got sober—I honestly thought I wasn't saved until I had stopped drinking completely. That was wrong. The truth is, I was saved from the time I believed Jesus as a boy. My mind simply needed to be renewed to the truth of who I am.

Terrible teaching made me *think* "stopping sinning" was the goal to prove my salvation. Quitting heavy drinking was on that list of works. A person can attempt to clean up their life all they want, even as an unbeliever. They still need Christ's life. This is what proves our salvation. *His* life and nothing else because *His* life never ends (see Hebrews 7:24-25, John 3:16).

Poor preaching has contorted the minds of many Christians to focus on behavior. Those who struggle with self-righteousness will hurl stones, "So Matt, are you saying we can just sin?!"

Yeah. That's exactly what I'm saying. Paul said all things are permissible but not all things are beneficial (see 1 Corinthians 10:23). You *can* sin but in your heart you don't *want* to sin as a believer. Go ahead and sin, watch what happens. The Spirit within you will reveal every time, "This is not for you."

You'll always walk away unfulfilled, even if you're in denial you'll know because you're an actual child of God. You can't get away from your sinless identity, your righteousness. You're a slave to it and you'll be perpetually convicted of your holiness:

"You have been set free from sin and have become slaves to righteousness."
(Romans 6:18)

I still experience such supernatural counsel just not with drinking. Now it's different sins. I may not be getting smashed, blowing money on booze, or making dumb drunk decisions, but I still fail. The lie, "Yes! That's what you want!" gets me all the time because I really *don't* want to sin. I want what God wants and I'll prove this by walking according to my true nature or by denying myself as a reborn saint (see Galatians 5:17).

SIN DOES NOT MAKE SENSE TO ME! But I still choose it sometimes because I'm a human being. Thankfully when I do, God's grace abounds (see Romans 5:20, 2 Corinthians 12:9).

I might get a flash-in-the-pan thrill—a fleshy kick—but emptiness is what my spirit experiences each time I fake who I am. Sometimes this remorse happens immediately, and sometimes the following week, month, or year. But anything that is not of faith will never set right with me. I'm a new creation who houses God Almighty—this I can't refute (see Romans 14:23, 1 Corinthians 6:19, 2 Corinthians 5:17, Colossians 1:22, 2 Peter 1:4).

We are free to choose to sin without having our sinful choices count against us. That's the entire basis of the gospel (see 1 Corinthians 10:23, 2 Corinthians 5:19, Acts 20:24). Think about it, what would happen if we do sin? Which we will, a lot. The answer is *we're forgiven*. John pens this truth:

> *"I am writing to you, little children, <u>because your sins have been forgiven</u> you for His name's sake." (1 John 2:12)*

This is called *grace* and grace infuriates those who don't see the Cross for all it's truly worth. Grace causes many behavior-centered people to plot the demise of another.

"It's not fair! They aren't getting away with this! There *is* a point where Christians run out of grace and *we* get what *we* deserve!"

No friend, there's not. Our sins are not more powerful than the blood of Messiah. Grace abounds. When we mess up we *never* get what we deserve from God. We might from planet earth and the people on it, but not from our Creator. With Him, we only get what Christ deserves (see 2 Corinthians 5:21, Colossians 3:24).

If you don't believe Jesus, yes, unfortunately you'll get exactly what you deserve. The Bible says our best efforts are like filthy rags; it warns us, we must be perfect like Jesus if we want to be judged according to our actions and attitudes *apart* from Him (see Isaiah 64:6, Matthew 5:48, 7:21-23). No human has ever been graded on a curve on their Day of Judgment. It's pass or fail, sheep or goat (see Matthew 25:31-33, Revelation 20:11-15).

For Christians, here's how we'll be judged because of our one-time faith in the Cross:

Repeated sins? Forgiven.
Lifelong sins? Forgiven.
Random sins? Forgiven.

To God, there aren't different levels of sins; absolute perfection is required (see Hebrews 10:14). All sins deserve death, from gossip to murder (see Romans 6:23). Jesus died. He won't die for our sins ever again. This is where our identity truly lies. That is, in what *He's* done.

So today, my friends, know this: My identity has never been in my recovery. During my binge drinking, each time I got drunk, I was already forgiven. Jesus' blood had taken away *all* my sins, not just my sins of debauchery. Even my future sins were forgiven and they still are because all my sins were in the future when Christ died for them. This is the foundation I needed to stand on. I needed to stop *trying* to express my sobriety and just be myself. How simple. Whatever your struggle may be, Christian, stop struggling. Stop finding your identity *in* the struggle or lack thereof. Just be you and rest in your forgiveness. God takes it from there.

A prayer for you: *Good morning Heavenly Father, what a beautiful sunrise you've given me. As I glance out these windows I'm amazed at your artwork of color, wildlife, trees and sky. You're such an amazing artist but your creativity pales in comparison to your grace. I thank you for it. Right now, I lift up all who are reading this, directly to you. Dad, help them to refocus on who you've remade them to be. Whatever distraction they're facing today, remind them who they are, or who they can be, if they'll place their faith in Jesus, once. These dear believers are your sinless children. They are slaves to nothing except for righteousness. In Christ's name I pray, amen.*

Day 12

The #1 Problem of Today's Church

"But I have this against you: You have abandoned your first love."

Revelation 2:4

We've lost sight of our first love in our churches: *Jesus.*

As a result, many Sunday gatherings are extremely damaging to the souls of patrons. Because the "devout" have taken their gaze off Christ, the New Covenant isn't being taught. Instead, a mixture of Law and grace is. Legalists attempt to water-down the Law and then pressure others to obey it like them. On Sundays—and Wednesdays if you're *really* holy—you'll get trained up on this.

They absolutely *refuse* to hold the Law to its highest standard as Christ commanded—perfection (see Matthew 5:48)—and then, repent toward grace. These addicts of religion are the ones *truly* not respecting the Law. We actually are. *We* are saying, "I can't do that! 613 commandments or none? I'll stick with Jesus!"

They are not. They want *parts* of Law and *parts* of grace, but God won't allow it. We must decide—one or the other—because Law plus grace is still Law (see Romans 7:4-5, 11:6, Galatians 5:18, Hebrews 7:19).

To be clear, yes, fellowship with other believers is important, but it's better to stay home than to repeatedly hear mixed-Covenant messages. Law-based sermons and treatments, such as:

1. "Do more, be more, try harder!"
2. "You're a sinner *and* a saint, so you better fight yourself and die daily!"
3. "Give until it hurts!"
4. "Tithe if you want to be blessed! To achieve *great* wealth, give an offering *above* the tithe!"
5. "Never question Pastor! If you do, hit the road, because he's more godly than you!"
6. "Our pastor has *two* seminary degrees and he's a *master* in linguistics! Fall in line, listen to him, and shut up! He's never wrong!"
7. "You better please God *more*! He'll turn His back on you if you *don't* serve!"
8. "Be careful to not make idols of anything—lest you fall!"—which *this* theology causes you to question everything and everyone you enjoy, so *then* you make an idol of *not* making idols!

...Oy vey.

This catastrophe, located in *so* many churches, is rampant and not the gospel. Yet millions will hear this trash because, "Don't you *dare* forsake the assembly of one another!"—a person yells, taking Hebrews 10:25 way out of context, which had nothing to do with church attendance (read the whole chapter). It's as if stepping inside a building to hear this dung is supposed to make us more sanctified and acceptable to God? It does not.

Go fishing, play golf, read, write, knit, spend time with your family. Kiss your spouse on the couch. Drink some coffee or tea and relax. Drive the countryside and enjoy the beautiful vistas. Do *anything* except go to church if this is what you experience each week.

You are free, friend. So *live* free.

It was for freedom that Christ set you free. Don't allow yourself to be burdened again by the yoke of sanctimonious slavery (see Galatians 5:1, Romans 5:1, Matthew 11:28-30).

"Remember the Sabbath and keep it holy!" they'll harp, applying one of the 613 commands for the Jews only *to us* while overlooking the fact that the Sabbath was not on Sunday. It was from Friday to Saturday. So who's *really* not keeping the Sabbath holy? Them. The Law-lovers. Those who crucify Christ again and again. We Christians have repented from a specific holy day and turned to Jesus as our holiness—*as* our Sabbath (see Colossians 2:16, Matthew 12:8, Hebrews 4:9-11, 6:6).

"God created the Sabbath for man, not the other way around," Jesus' own words (see Mark 2:27).

In some churches, many drink from the toilet of legalism and try to shove the heads of others down into the same pot. They want *us* to believe our Creator gives gold stars on our *Good Little Christian Chart* for putting our butts in the pews and listening to lies. No. It doesn't work that way. We must stand up to this. We need to recenter our gatherings onto the truth of the simplicity of the gospel:

JUST JESUS. He is enough.

The number one problem with our assemblies is the mixture of the Old and New Covenants. Moses *plus* Jesus. Law *plus* grace. If Paul could see what we're doing by *not* being clear about Christians being dead to the Law—100% *no* relationship with it—he'd call us, "Fools!" (See Galatians 3:1). The double-talkers who are teaching a mixture, he'd tell them to castrate themselves (see Galatians 5:12).

That's how serious he was.

"STOP MIXING IN THE LAW WITH THE GOSPEL!"

But we don't like to listen to that. We think we need the Law, when we don't, *because* we have the Spirit. We'll trust Jesus for His blood and forgiveness but stonewall at trusting His Spirit to guide us choice by choice—as if He's silent or something. He's not (see Galatians 5:22-23, Hebrews 1:2, Philippians 4:8, 1 Corinthians 2:16, 13:1-13, 2 Corinthians 3:7-9, 10:5, John 13:34, 14:26).

This will infuriate someone who's worked way too hard at being obedient to the Law—parts of it anyway, "You're a liar, Matt! Without the commandments from Moses how will we know what to do?!"

Jesus. Him. His Spirit. He's infused with *your* spirit, believer (see 1 Corinthians 6:17). *He* teaches you, not Moses (see John 1:17, Titus 2:11-12, Galatians 3:24). He'll never lead you into sin, don't worry. You can still choose to sin, but that's not coming from Him. That's coming from the power of sin, demonic influences, and your own unrenewed thoughts and coping mechanisms. You'll know what to do on a moment by moment basis because of His Spirit *not* because of the Law.

But no, many think He's not suffice and His grace is useless. For this reason, they won't center their teachings on Him. Jesus is just a footnote to their incorrect opinion *about* Him. Confused pastors will pull stuff He said out of context—as well as the things Paul wrote—and *everything* Moses commanded. Their weak "Top Ten" they'll fight tooth and nail for, in order to keep some obsolete stone tablets on their courthouse square. Yet *all of them* fail miserably at obeying *even* the Ten Commandments and *still* pressure others to do them! Talk about *hypocrites*! That's exactly what Law observance does, which was *exactly* the point of the Law from the beginning:

EXPOSE THE SELF-RIGHTEOUS, GRACELESS, GODLESS, FAITHLESS HYPOCRITES.
(See Romans 3:9,20, 5:20, 6:14, Matthew 23:1-37, James 2:10, Galatians 2:19, 3:10-11)

No matter, they'll ignore this truth and scream, "Not one jot or tittle can be ignored!" Well no duh, but those jots and tittles only apply to unbelievers, not Christians. Paul told Timothy the same; that the Law is not for us. Instead, it's for those who are not born of the Spirit, *natural* sinners (see 1 Timothy 1:7-11).

WE ARE NOT SINNERS! WE ARE CHILDREN OF GOD! CHILDREN OF GOD DO NOT NEED THE LAW! (See 1 John 3:1, Romans 6:14).

THE LAW IS THE *POWER* OF SIN! PLEASE STOP PUTTING PEOPLE UNDER IT! (See 1 Corinthians 15:56).

Dear preacher, do you *want* sin? Do you want sin to be *powerful* in your congregation? Then dip your teachings into the Law. Cover Moses with Jesus and create candy-coated crap, then hand it out each week. Watch the place get sick and fall apart. Go ahead, just use a dollop, just *one* commandment from the Old Testament, then sit back and observe demonic gremlins go to work. Put a *drop* of poison into the spiritual food you feed your flock and watch sin *thrive* (see Galatians 5:9, Romans 7:8,11).

Or repent and teach Christ. Repent and teach the Spirit as our Guide, not Law. Repent and stop pointing out, "What all is wrong with the ministries of others who are easy on sin." Repent and teach complete reconciliation with God. STOP FOCUSING ON SIN. Focus on Jesus. Truth be told, that's the only thing we're *all* competent to teach:

100% RECONCILIATION WITH GOD THROUGH CHRIST.
(See 2 Corinthians 5:11-21)

Context-contortion of Old and New Covenants has ruined countless churches. We're hard-pressed to find New Covenant teachings coming from any pulpit. The mixture of Jesus and Moses has caused quasi-grace country clubs to pop up everywhere; congregations instructed to inspect peoples' fruits when Jesus only mentioned fruit inspection as He chastised some unbelieving jerks—not us. For us, it's *His* fruit being produced *through* us. We are simply branches. He is the vine. Branches don't produce, we rest. The vine does the work by way of us (see John 15:5, Galatians 5:22-23, Philippians 2:13).

So today, my friends, know this: The number one problem of today's church is the message. The message we hear isn't centered on Jesus *in* us and *through* us. It's riddled with unnecessary garbage which pulls our attention off Him. We must repent back *toward* our first love, Christ alone and His grace. Covenant-mixing churches pervade our planet when Paul clearly stated the Letter kills. The Letter is the Law (see 2 Corinthians 3:6). The Law is the Old Covenant between God and Israel, yet many pastors want to tell people to give the Law their best shot and come back next week for a new, convicting pep-talk. No! Repent! Christ is *for* you, friend! Paul said the Spirit gives life! He said the only message anyone is competent to teach *is* the New Covenant! He said we're *all* ministers of it, not just those who deacon boards vote into supposed power (see 2 Corinthians 3:6). That's you, dear Christian! You are qualified to minister the New Covenant because the Spirit who gave you life lives in you! (See 1 Corinthians 6:19, Hebrews 3:6).

A prayer for you: *Father, thank you so much for another day alive! Thank you for your Spirit within me! Right now, I lift up all who are reading this, directly to you. Please help our church gatherings to turn from the Law and back toward Jesus. Yes, they can know the Law, they can learn the history of Israel and the lineage of our Savior. But more importantly, they need to know where WE came in—the Cross. The blood of Jesus brought in the New Covenant and that's where human history changed for the better. Inform them that Moses, David, Daniel, Jeremiah—all of Israel—longed for what we now have! Since Pentecost, Christ's very own Spirit joins all who will believe! He's guiding us, counseling us, and teaching us how to live our lives every second of the day! He's our only hope of glory and we have Him in full as your children! Guide our churches into repentance, right back to our first love, Jesus. In His name I pray, amen.*

Day 13

Can Christians Have Boundaries?

"If it is possible, as far as it depends on you, live at peace with everyone."

Romans 12:18

Boundaries are so important. As a Christian, legalism and guilt can cause us to think we're not allowed to have boundaries. Many will attempt to take advantage of our identity, as if we're to be overlooked, our feelings ignored, and if we don't like it?

"Tough! Turn the other cheek and deal with it! You're a Christian! What would Jesus do?!"

This is wrong and not from God. Such notions are actually from the enemy and the power of sin (see Revelation 12:10, Genesis 4:7). First of all, *we* are not God, we're human. Therefore our relationships with other humans isn't the same as God's relationship with them. So our *human* relationships can't be compared in all aspects; that is, like God's with people.

For example, we humans like to be apologized to when someone hurts us, this is reasonable and healthy. Forgiveness is *ongoing* with us and others. With God it isn't because He only forgives through blood and Christ does not shed His blood *ongoingly*. It's finished. He did this once and won't do it again. *People* aren't offering blood to us for forgiveness. That'd be gross. When someone says, "I'm sorry," building trust can begin again, not when they say, "Here, take this blood."

Do you see the difference? God has a blood-based forgiveness system. We have an apology-based forgiveness system. Yes, we can still forgive without an apology, but to build a strong union apologies sure do help.

With God, we can apologize all we like but apologies don't forgive us. Any unbeliever can apologize, they still need a one-time faith in Christ. Again, our Creator only forgives by way of faith in blood *once* in our entire lifetime. Our mustard-seed-size confidence in Jesus' blood allows us to access the Father and Son's faithfulness to each other. We become beneficiaries to *their* promise to one another, established at the Cross (see Hebrews 6:16-19, 9:16,22-24, 10:10-14, 1 John 2:2, John 3:16-18, 19:30, 2 Timothy 2:13).

We can and should say sorry to God, but never to be repeatedly forgiven. Jesus will never die again so we will never be forgiven again as believers (see Hebrews 1:3, 7:25).

Therefore, in regard to healthy boundaries, as Christians, we're allowed to establish them with people for our own well-being. No matter what flavor of guilt is placed on us—aggressive or passive-aggressive—God encourages us to enjoy our lives peacefully. We can only do this with others through boundaries. Paul tells the Romans:

"If it is possible, as far as it depends on you, live at peace with everyone."
(Romans 12:18)

It's not always possible to live at peace with everyone. Their disrespectful boundary-crossing won't allow it. Sometimes it's religious boundary-crossing, such as a pastor or sanctimonious aunt pushing Law on you. Other times, it's in your own home, such as a lazy individual who won't get out of bed, or a spouse not honoring their marriage vows. It could even be a friend or grandchild who continually mooches off you.

No boundaries equals no living at peace. No boundaries equals no enjoyment of a relationship. Instead, chaos, pain, disorganization, codependency, abuse, filth, and frustration is the result.

Someone might say, "We don't need boundaries, we have Jesus," and that's true. Jesus is enough. This is why He'll never lead us to allow ourselves to be repeatedly hurt. His Holy Spirit will guide us toward establishing boundaries for our own well-being. This isn't selfish, it's wise. We cannot express Christ without taking care of ourselves, so we must stand up to ongoing poor treatment.

To be clear, boundaries are not ultimatums or even threats. Boundaries aren't rude or out of control. Boundaries aren't brick walls, they don't shut people out. Healthy boundaries are always established in love, both for you *and* the other person. Boundaries are where you begin and others end, and vice versa.

Here are some examples of what boundaries look like:

"That won't work for me."
"I've changed my mind."
"I won't be attending because when I do I don't feel comfortable."
"I feel attacked and manipulated, so I'll not be involved with that any longer."
"You can't speak to my child that way, even if you *are* the coach, that won't work. You need to respect them."

"Your addiction is impacting our family negatively. Please get help with this. We love you and need you to be healthy."

"That's not okay."

"Don't touch me."

"You're not allowed to talk to me that way."

"You're not allowed to treat me like that, it hurts."

"Your flirting on social media must stop."

"I need to know the passcode on your phone."

"That relationship needs to end because it harms our marriage and isn't appropriate."

"This must change because I love you, and because I love myself too."

"You don't get to decide how I run my business."

"You don't get to decide how I raise my children."

"If you won't help out, you need to leave."

"If you won't respect our home, you can't come over."

"There's too much heavy drinking going on there. I don't want to be around that."

"You can't just stop by anytime you like. This causes our evening to be out of whack. Please ask first."

"Please don't call and expect me to talk for a long period of time. I'll be glad to speak to you when I'm caught up with my responsibilities for the day."

"Private time with my spouse is important to me. You're welcome here, but please don't interrupt our evenings together by staying past 8pm, or by coming over every single day."

"I will not loan you any money. The last loan I gave you, you never paid back. I work hard and you keep taking advantage of me. This stops now."

"No."

Boundaries are *your* responsibility for *you,* never for the other person. You cannot force someone to create their own boundaries nor respect yours, but you *can* create consequences—out of love—when others cross your boundaries. Boundaries do not automatically end a relationship on your part. In fact, they're meant to bring the relationship closer and ultimately strengthen it by saying, "These are my needs."

Boundaries are see-through fences with gates which let people in and show them out. Those gates also allow *us* to take out our *own* garbage but *we* are not the garbage, nor are the boundary-crossers.

Without boundaries, it's easy to be drained and we can easily become addicted to fixing others—which is impossible. Without boundaries, anxiety thrives, enabling flourishes, our self-worth is neglected, and our feelings belittled. We need boundaries, even as Christians. In my opinion, *especially* as Christians.

So today, my friends, know this: You are worth boundary establishments! God never called us to be martyrs, but ambassadors! (See 2 Corinthians 5:20). Ambassadors should be strong and confident! Boundaries will help you represent Jesus in great ways by showing others your true value! Take time to talk with God about how to establish healthy boundaries. He longs to give you insight. Never allow pressure, shame, or anger from others to erase your boundaries. Never allow your feelings to be ignored! Your feelings are important! Address people with kindness as you learn to establish boundaries which are meant to help you *enjoy* your life! Your quality of life matters!

A prayer for you: *Father, thank you for teaching me that boundaries are a good thing. For so long, I allowed completely unacceptable behavior from others due to the fact that I witnessed enabling growing up. I, myself, also crossed many boundaries through my own poor choices and attitudes. Thank you for maturing me, it's helped so much! Right now, I lift up all who are reading this, directly to you. So many of these dear people have been legalistically abused into thinking they can't have boundaries as a Christian. They think YOU want them to allow abuse, in order to prove their humility and holiness. Reveal that these are lies. Your words in the Bible have been twisted into causing them to believe they must constantly be taken advantage of. That is, to prove their faith. Let them know this is from hell, not from you, Father. You care for your children and don't want them hurt. Take them deeper into the truth of just how valuable they are to you—SO valuable, Jesus died for them! As they grow in understanding their immense worth, the unhealthy connections will die off, or improve, and new ones will prosper! Guide them moment by moment as they learn! In Christ's name, amen.*

Day 14

The Top Ten Lies About God's Will

"Therefore do not be foolish, but understand what the Lord's will is."

Ephesians 5:17

Satan, rubbing his hands together, speaks, "If I can just keep them confused about God's will, their lives will be ruined. If they'll *just* believe my lies about what He wants for them, their relationships will fall apart! They'll constantly question their choice of job, spouse, where they live, their salvation, and they'll be anxious all the time! They'll never have peace with the decisions they've made *if* I can befuddle them about the will of God!"

The author of confusion—Lucifer—has the most to say about God's will, and many have believed him. Thankfully, God's will is simple. It's Jesus. It's the Spirit of Jesus in you and through you. How elementary. How *not* confusing.

Paul Ellis, author and friend of mine, wrote this:

> "Not everything that happens is God's will. If everything that happens is God's will, then it's God's will for me to tell you that not everything is God's will."

Does that make sense? Do you see what he did there? He simplified something Satan and religious people have made overbearingly difficult. Dark forces and the uber-sanctimonious have caused many to live in a perpetual state of paralysis of analysis. Some can't even go to the grocery store without obsessing about God's will for each individual purchase. I'm serious. This is a *real* thing.

With all due respect, for these squirrels caught in the middle of the road, when a *big* decision appears, they instantly turn to stone. Unable to decide, "Do I go left, or right?!" all because they can't "hear" from God. As a result they freeze and don't know what to do.

"I've made too many mistakes in the past by not listening to God's will for me! I'm not doing that again!"

"SPEAK TO ME GOD! WHY ARE YOU SILENT?! SPEEEEEEAK!"

"Everything is screwed up because I had so much sin in my life I *couldn't* hear from God! The pastor told me so!"

"It's my fault I'm at where I'm at! I ignored God's will, therefore I missed my calling!"

I've been building up to write this devotional for about a year and a half now. With six published books and having a social media "memistry," I get asked quite often, "Do you have anything on the will of God?"

I didn't want to rush this topic so I've mostly stayed vague. Although in my spirit I knew the truth, I never felt like I had enough information to be thorough. That is, in using my gift of creative writing to attempt to explain such a thing.

What most people don't know is that after each devotional I write, I'll post it on social media before I put it in a book. I pay close attention to the feedback, then I'll edit it by adding in concerns and questions I may have missed. I doubt I'll have missed any for this devotional. At this point I have *too* much info on the topic.

In October of 2018, I began stockpiling primary questions, comments, quotes, memes, private messages, Bible passages, and blatant lies about God's will. In front of me I now have a nice, neat, stack of notes. If you could see this small mountain of short writings, emails to myself, and cut-out memes sitting here on my ottoman, you'd understand that this subject could become a short book. Why?

Because God's desires for us is immensely important to us.

There's not enough time to write all this out. Rather, I've come up with the top ten lies, in no particular order, based on my copious amount of research. I truly hope this list gives you confidence and peace in knowing the simplicity of God's will for you. Enjoy.

1. **"God's will is that you *not* have grief."** This lie is directed toward those who are grieving "too long." As these dear people suffer with severe grief—such as the death of a loved one, loss of a job or marriage—insensitive individuals attempt to push them *past* their supposed stop-clock of mourning. As if God wants them to, "Hurry up and not be sad!" No! That's a lie. Bottling up feelings will only cause worse things to happen. The truth is, grief is a *feeling* and God gave us the ability to feel for a reason. There's no time limit in Scripture to be quick to feel things, or slow. Feelings allow us to express what's going on in our soul. There's not a single passage in the Bible which commands us to *not* feel something or *to* feel something. We're allowed to feel what we feel as long as we feel it. God never pressures us to change

our feelings, especially grief. Instead, He comforts us in the hallows of our deep pain. Never does He say, "Don't grieve so much!" or "Get with it! Stop mourning already! Where is your faith?!" Alternatively, He gently expresses to our spirit, "My sweet child, take as much time as you need. I'm with you in this. You're never alone." (See Revelation 21:4, Psalm 34:18, Matthew 5:4, Hebrews 13:5).

2. **"I've dropped out of God's will because of a huge sin from my past."** If I were putting these in order this would be number one. This lie, sold by the devout, is why countless people give up on going deeper into their relationship with Jesus. Numerous messages I've received prove many Christians believe they've blown it. Due to a pretentious person deceiving them, "Look at your lifestyle! You've lived like hell and you called yourself a Christian! You've not repented well enough!" many children of God accept this falsity as gospel. Here's what the behavior-police have convinced them of: "There are many different *levels* of sinning! Big sins will drop you out of God's will! It's too late for you!" The reality is, there are *not* different levels of sinning on this side of the Cross. Sadly, those who don't understand what Jesus completed by His death and resurrection will dip back into the Old Covenant and use Proverbs 6:16-19 to cherry-pick "the worst" sins. "THESE ARE ABOMINATIONS! THIS IS WHAT GOD HATES!" However, the truth is, God hates *every* sin and *every* sin deserves death—not just these few. And, we live on *this* side of the Cross which means *everything* which is *not* of faith is sin. From gossiping, to gluttony, to murdering 50 people, every sin *requires* death. Not repenting, but death. Sin does not require the silent treatment from God about His will for your life. It requires *death.* Jesus died. If we get our calculators out and do the math, His *single* death paid off all our sins *once* for all our life. How? Because He's not bound by time. No

sin could ever keep us out of God's will, which is Christ, He's hidden us inside of Himself. (See 2 Peter 3:8, Romans 1:29-31, 6:23, 14:23, Hebrews 1:3, 10:10-14, Colossians 3:3).

3. **"If it's God's will, it will happen. We don't need to do anything except wait on Him."** I once heard a story about a man drowning in the ocean. "Help me, God! Help me! I'm going to die! I can't swim, Lord!" he shouted. Soon enough a boat comes by, "Here, take this lifesaver!" the deckhand yells. "Grab it and I'll pull you in!" Strangely, the man replies, "No! I'm waiting on God!" So the boat faded off into the distance. Three minutes later another ship offers support. With only his chin above water, the man squeaks, "God's got me! Go on!" As soon as it sails away he goes under, drowns, and dies. Immediately appearing in heaven, he asks God, "Why didn't you save me?" God grins, chuckles, then retorts, "I sent you two boats, silly. You should've taken their help." Friend, we are not puppets, we are *people*. God doesn't *want* anyone to perish, but we must believe in the one whom He has sent, Jesus. And when He clearly offers us help through others, we should accept it. Don't sit still and drown, reach out and receive their gift of help. (See 2 Peter 3:9, John 3:16, Galatians 6:7-10).
4. **"If I read my Bible, do devotions, and go to church, *then* I'll unlock God's will for my life."** If this were true, what would happen if you could no longer read—or you never *could* read? What if you no longer had the *time* to do devotions? What if you're not the type of person who wants to sit still and read because it's not in your personality? What if you weren't physically able to go to a church building, or you live in a country where it's not allowed, or your right to go to church is taken away? Friend, you'd worry about God's will, that's what would happen. Worry is not from God. Do you see how these things do not cause God's will nor maintain it? Sure, such can be wonderful

in helping us mature, as long as Christ is the focus, but God's will is never unlocked through anything we do or don't do. (See Luke 12:25, Matthew 11:28-30, Galatians 5:1).

5. **"Prayer is not forcing God to do your will but preparing you to do His will."** Jesus prayed, "Not my will, but your will be done," before He was betrayed. However, He was praying from the view of His humanity. He is God, but at the same time He knew the physical pain He was about to endure to pay off our sins. Clearly, His will is the same as the Father and the Spirit's—they are one. So when someone uses this verse to make us believe our will is not the same as God's will until we pray and He changes it? That's off base for Christians. We are not pitted against God in lieu of prayer. That's worse than having an accountability partner; we would avoid praying like we avoid *them*. Yes, through prayer the Spirit reveals things, sometimes instantly, sometimes later. He gently reminds us about making wise, righteous decisions; common sense surfaces in our thoughts. Through inspiration and motivation He'll direct us toward advocates, mature friends, counselors, and Christian family members to consult with in our times of trouble. As we pray, every so often obvious writing-on-the-wall which matches up to both *your* will *and* God's transpires. We *know*. We aren't being prepared to do anything different from what God wants, nor what *we* truly want. (See Luke 22:42, John 14:26, Galatians 5:22-23, 1 Corinthians 2:16, 13:4-8).
6. **"We can frustrate the will of God."** If this were true, God would not be God. It's impossible to frustrate the Omniscient One. Everything God was frustrated about was put on Christ at the Cross. Take a glance at the Old Testament and you'll see how *furiously* frustrated He was. To be clear, sure, we can frustrate religious people and demons who put pressure on us, but not God. THE CROSS WAS A HUGE

SUCCESS. BLAME JESUS, NOT ME. So now, God works in us and through us, never frustrated but encouraging and loving, even while correcting us. (See Luke 1:37, Romans 5:1,9).

7. **"If you didn't *fully* give your will to God, you're not really saved."** This is wrong because our will doesn't keep us saved, our new heart does. Christ staying alive allows us to *have* our new heart. At salvation, through an act of our will *once*, we fully gave God our wicked heart. I REPEAT, FULLY. He then *fully* gave us back a new heart which is forever protected by the life of Christ. A legalist who wants to define *fully* by their own works will shout, "No way, Matt! I've seen people in church for fifteen years who walked away from God because their *full* will wasn't ever *really* involved, and it didn't *stay* involved!" The truth is, if they were ever saved during those fifteen years, once, what *fully* happened is they walked away from people teaching this trash, not God. I'm happy for them. (See Ezekiel 36:26, Colossians 3:4, Romans 6:17, Hebrews 7:23-25).
8. **"God's will is like a dartboard with a bullseye. If you try hard enough, you can hit the center, but if not, you'll never get the best from His will."** Wow. Just typing that sentence, memories of religious abuse gets stirred up in my soul. Many who don't understand Jesus have split God's will up into sections and placed the emphasis on *us* to throw "our dart." Demonic forces have labeled this *permissive will* and *perfect will*. Friend, there is no dartboard. There was a Cross. God permitted this flawless sacrifice for us. Jesus hung on the bullseye, the center of it, and we benefit *perfectly* from God's will by placing our faith in Him once.
9. **"God's will is that you suffer! So suck it up and carry your cross!"** What we've believed about this lie has caused more physical, mental, emotional, and sexual abuse than we can possibly calculate.

Wolves in sheep's clothing love this lie because it allows them to control you. I agree, 1 Peter 3:17 says, *"For it is better, if it is God's will, to suffer for doing good than for doing evil."* But many have twisted this into, "It's God's will that you suffer!" No flipping way. Peter's point is, "Behave, and if you suffer while behaving, you are doing God's will." Remember, it was God's will that Christ suffer, not you. Just read around Peter's statement for context. The church was being persecuted and Pete was saying, "Keep doing good things! God is with you!" As for carrying our cross? Jesus said this to the disciples informing them of what they *couldn't* do and what only *He* could do. He was exposing their need for *His* sacrifice at *His* Cross—not their own. On this side of Calvary we *have been* crucified, with Him! This happened! WE'VE COME BACK FROM THE DEAD! We are not on that Cross with Him any longer! That was Friday! WE CAME OUT OF THE TOMB! We are not repeatedly dying! We live forever! When Paul said, "I die daily," he was talking about the physical dangers he faced as he traveled—not himself! There's no more cross to bear! We are alive! We are not called to suffer but to fully live an abundant life in Christ! (See Isaiah 53:10, Galatians 2:20, Romans 6:3-11, Colossians 3:1-4, 1 Corinthians 15:30-32, 2 Corinthians 5:17-21, John 10:10).

10. **"You can easily get outside of God's will by making bad decisions, and if you do, you better repent quickly!"** This is the type of lie which causes people to hate Christians because it creates stress and fear in others. It's almost the same as number two on this list but this lie is a *repeated* dropping out of God's will. It causes a person to stay in a ceaseless state of panic, even over their thoughts. Then, to get back into God's will they must act fast! They gotta *do* something or *see* someone or *go* to a geographical location. They *think* they're failures yet they aren't. They're safe in God's will forever no matter what

> choices they make for the rest of their lives. The truth is, every decision—good, bad, or indifferent—has no bearing on God's will staying intact. Who do we think we are? How can *we* override the Creator of the universe and His great love for us in Christ? "What should I do, God? I'll wait for a sign! I'll wait for confirmation so that my next decision is yours!" No, friend, don't do that. Rest instead. We simply need rest and *live*. We simply need to *be*. We simply need to *trust* as a baby jumping off the edge of a pool directly into their smiling father's arms. God is a good Father and He allows us to decide where we live, who to be involved with romantically, what job to take, how many kids to have, what car to buy, whether to have a ministry or not—whatever, all of it. During each stage of our life *we* choose *what* to do and He goes *with* us. He's never disappointed and never leaves. Disappointments, to Him, are called sins. Jesus has removed those already so don't worry. He's looked down the timeline of your life and decided to forgive you of everything. It's never too late to enjoy Him in whatever you've decided to do with your life. With anything, with everything, and with everyone, we're always in His will, Christian. We're always in Jesus.

So today, my friends, know this: God's will is that we give thanks in all things; not thanking Him *for* the bad things, but thanks for Him being with us *during* the bad things. God's will is to rescue us, that none perish, and all come to understand the knowledge of His Son. God's will is not that we surrender, but to be reborn. We are never commanded to surrender in Scripture, but to be reborn into His family by grace through faith. God's will is to give us wisdom and to have our minds renewed to the truth of Christ in us, guiding us. God's will is that we mature and grow into who we truly are. God's will isn't always easy, according to our old methods of coping, but it's always perfect, according to our new identity. God's will is to work in us and through us, to fulfill His good purposes. God's will is both the Jew and the Gentile join Him as the New Creation. God's will is that we express Him and bear much fruit. God's will is to give *us* glory, the same glory He had before Adam and Eve were created. God's will is Christ in us and us in Him—oneness. God's will is for us to be protected by the promise between the Father and Son made at the Cross.

All these things can be found in Jesus. Therefore, God's will is Jesus.

(See 1 Thessalonians 5:18, 2 Peter 3:9, Ephesians 1:7, Romans 9-11, 12:2, Philippians 2:13, Galatians 3:28, 6:15, John 14:20, 15:8, 17:22-23, 19:30, Colossians 1:26-27, 1 Corinthians 6:17-19, Hebrews 6:16-19)

A prayer for you: *Dad, thank you for letting me call you Dad. Your will is to allow me to do this. Romans 8 tells me I can call you Abba, which means Daddy. Daddy means Dad. This was your exact will for me, to be your son. Your will is my will, I can never step out of this, on purpose nor accidentally. Thank you for making me righteous like you and guiding my righteous plans. Proverbs 12:5 tells me whatever I decide to do, I'm still righteous. I know I still make unrighteous choices sometimes, but you're still with me, working all things out for good. Right now, I lift up all who are reading this, directly to you. Many of these dear readers are confused and scared about your will. Anxiety riddles their lives about what decisions to make and when. Give them a sense of peace today. Remind them that angst isn't coming from you. Your divine will is clear. It's Christ in them, and if they have Him, they're enjoying your will at all times. They have*

NOT missed the boat. If they want to move to another city, or country, they are free! If they want to stay put—THEY ARE FREE! Let them also know your will is that we are healed SPIRITUALLY through Christ. Yes, you perform miracles, but those are rare for a reason. This planet is not where we belong permanently. Assure them, Father, that you'll never leave them. If they're prostituting on the street, binge drinking in a bar, or shooting up heroin in their bedroom, your will is to be with them—and you are. If they're struggling as a legalistic pastor, a depressed missionary, or abused housewife commanded to constantly submit, your will is to be with them—and you are. Rich or poor, in sickness or good health, your will is contentment in all things. Your will is your grace being sufficient. Your will is to let us decide, and to be with us, through Jesus. We are grateful. In His holy name I pray, amen.

Day 15

Gentleness and Respect

"Always be prepared to give an answer to everyone who asks you to give the reason for the hope that you have. But do this with gentleness and respect"

See 1 Peter 3:15

We live in a world of social media. It's very sad, but some people, even Christians, are looking for an opportunity to pounce onto others online:

"You're an idiot and should know better."
"You're just looking to hide sins from God!"
"You have no right to be speaking about God. You need to study yourself approved! Reach out for wise counsel from a godly man!"
"Well my Bible says *this*!"

Rude, aggressive, insensitive comments can even come from those who have a Bible verse at the top of their page. It's no wonder why the body of Christ has such a bad reputation. It's because we aren't expressing Him like we should.

As believers, the worst thing we can do is attack people for their beliefs or act like a know-it-all jerk toward those who are still learning the basics of Christ crucified. Sometimes, even when we know we're right, the best thing we can do is respond softly or be quiet in response to hateful remarks. No matter if those remarks are coming from contentious unbelievers or legalistic Christians *we* decide how we'll react.

Regrettably, there are even some who've become legalistic about the New Covenant. Information, information, information—"Shut up and listen," disguised by a delicate tone, is all they want to give others. Refusing to express any type of vulnerability or relatability, their attitude is, "These are the facts, deal with it. I have no interest in what you think. I'm right. You're wrong. Here's why."

These aren't safe people. We don't have to continually expose ourselves to them. We don't have to keep giving power to individuals who act like they don't love us. Even if they *say* they're teaching the New Covenant their sarcasm and arrogance is a blatant enemy of the Cross. No matter how many degrees they have it's gross when they attack others, especially when they make fun of someone's accent or struggles as they *attempt* to be funny on stage.

It's not funny. It's pretentious. Get some new jokes.

Some have become bodyguards for pastors who act like their role model in the pulpit is the Wizard of Oz. "He's my hero!" they bark.

"I thought Jesus was your hero?"

"Don't worry about me. Get in line and learn what you need to learn. Don't ever post, write, or say anything that sounds like my hero. God's grace affords me to tell you this. You'll only hear from me when I want something from you or when I need to correct your theology, and it will be via text or messenger. I'm not calling you."

Pastoral gatekeepers who act as if their minister is Christ Himself. Even those who fully understand the foundations of the New Covenant are doing this. What they fail to grasp is their pastor learned from another pastor before *them*. And those pastors before *them*. And *maybe* they didn't even learn the New Covenant truths *from* a pastor but from a regular person like me.

Who knows? Who cares? Ultimately it's the Spirit who reveals all truths, no matter who's expressing His message. Some need to step down from their high-horse and stop acting like a single person is God's gift to mankind. Jesus holds that title.

Placing one man's gifts higher than *all* things and *all* people? Protecting them with salty, uber-critical vigor? To me that sounds cultish. Too far? Probably, but so what. That's how I feel when someone lifts up a pastor higher than Christ, follows all your posts and stories, yet never comments unless it's to correct you or point out how their hero came up with the same idea *first*.

No, friend, the gospel is much older than your hero. The Spirit is eternal. He lives in *everyone* who believes. Those were *His* ideas, first.

I never thought I would see it but New Covenant cliques have formed. Count me out. Expressing legalism—not about Law, because they know we're dead to the Law—but about the New Covenant. Many are quick to point out where someone is lacking in truth—brutally—just the same as those who mix Law and grace. It's sanctimonious, just with a New Covenant hat on.

The issue is this:

THERE'S NO GENTLENESS OR RESPECT.

Peter said we should always be prepared to give an answer for the hope we have, but to do so gently and respectfully (see 1 Peter 3:15). Used to be, I'd go to war with anyone who was rude or aggressive, especially with a legalist or disrespectful unbeliever. But I dumped that immaturity a while back. If I find myself angry I won't respond at all. I'll set healthy boundaries to limit any future exposure to them. In some cases, with repeated disrespect, I'll dust my feet and move along for good. Most of the time I think nothing more about it and move forward to enjoy my day.

I don't even check to see who's my "friend" any longer, nor pay attention to who likes my posts. I refuse to be a slave to the opinion of others, even if they decide to electronically shut me out of their life. If I don't see someone's posts or likes pop up any longer? "Oh well, I wish them the best," is what I truly think.

It wasn't always like this. I'd get upset if I was unfriended or blocked. I'd also stay up until the wee hours of the morning going back and forth, trying to prove my point to others. I'd miss a whole day of work attempting to convince a person they're wrong and I'm right. Now, I don't need to be right. I need to enjoy my peace. I'll unfollow or even block a person if I see that my peace is in constant jeopardy. It's just not worth it.

The Holy Spirit has taught me there's plenty of people who actually *want* help and are searching for answers *kindly*. There are those who are willing to give me a chance to use *my* gifts to possibly steer them into the easiness of Christ. They are friends, and some aren't even Christians. What a concept, right? Unbelieving friends? Who would've thought of such a thing?

Social media calls people *friends* but most are not. They're *contacts* cloaked in a list of supposed friends. Really, it should be called a contact list not a friends list, but Facebook can make more money and collect more information from people when they cause us to believe we're gathering friends. Their frustrating algorithms don't even let you see your real friend's posts very often, but they sure as heck won't stop suggesting people you've never met.

The reality is, I have several true friends who know more than I do—in a scholarly way—yet they treat me with the utmost respect and care; not like a professor whom I have to constantly impress with no returned praise, and not like the intern for that professor who grades his papers.

I shouldn't be wasting my time, effort, thoughts, and energy on those who attack me, treat me like I'm some stupid Christian layman, or that there's something wrong with my ministry. I know what I need to know right now, at this exact moment in my life, just the same as I knew what I needed to know five years ago, at that exact moment in my life. I'm growing and maturing. We all are. None of us have made it to the peak of the Mountain of the Knowledge of God's Grace. We're not even supposed to be climbing it. We should be resting in the lush green pastures at the bottom of that mountain, in the valley with Jesus, being ourselves and enjoying our lives as saints.

Because Christ lives in me my knowledge is always good enough for God. He can use a donkey and illiterate fishermen to get His message out. He can use anyone or anything. I'm the first to admit that my grammar, spelling, punctuation, and theology isn't perfect, but my spirit is. My *God* is. And I'm one *with* Him. So are you, Christian (see Hebrews 10:10,14, 1 Corinthians 6:17).

I refuse to shrink back and *not* be who I am, no matter the flaws in my actions, attitudes, and learnedness. I'm going to do the best I can to be myself while resting in grace. I will ignore all discouragement, no matter if it's coming from Mosaic legalists or the New Covenant camp. I will set healthy boundaries to protect my mental well-being, confidence, and feelings.

My feelings *are* important, and so are yours, friend.

No matter where you're at in your walk, you too are enough for God! You too can do amazing things! If someone tells you otherwise don't believe it! Don't let anyone sway you from the dreams you have within!

Believer or not, when someone disagrees with us and they aren't attacking, we *should* consider engaging with them. After deciding to do this, over the years I've seen amazing results! Here's what I've learned:

1. **Pause and listen.** This seems simple, but God always leads us toward empathy and patience. If I find myself speeding up in order to make my point, this is a red flag to STOP. Expressing patience with others,

and with yourself, is much more important than knee-jerk, gotta-be-right reactions. We have nothing to prove. We simply have truth and love to share, Jesus. There's no pressure on us and life will go on even if we don't convince someone about Him. Christ saves, not us, so let others finish what they have to say and take a break.

2. **Don't tell people what to believe.** Easy enough, right? With religion and politics, the unfollow and mute buttons have become very popular. Rightfully so. Our feeds should be enjoyable! When others are constantly pushing us to believe a certain way, snooze them or unfollow them altogether. Take a step back from the group. *Leave* the group if it's ongoing. Juxtapose, with our evangelism, we don't want to be like the Pharisees, severely disrespecting people. They even killed others for not believing like them.
3. **Be sensitive.** Triple-check the things you post before you post it. What we put on social media is the same as putting it in the newspaper. Others *will* see it. Be sensitive to them, yourself, and those whom you love. Before posting, ask yourself: *Is this too personal? Will I feel the same tomorrow or next month? How will this impact my relationships, reputation, finances, and/or occupation? Am I dishonoring myself or someone who cares about me? Should I let my emotions calm down first?*
4. **Express gentleness and respect.** Again, 1 Peter 3:15 reminds us to be organic in our interactions. We're not faking these traits. We *are* gentle, we *are* respectful, we *are* new creations! (See 2 Corinthians 5:17, Galatians 5:22-23).
5. **Keep scrolling.** We don't have to comment on everything we disagree with. There's no peace in that. Let people express what's important to them. Some self-described devout Christians post things about God and our President which make me want to say, "Really?" But the truth is, they're allowed to have their own opinion and I'm allowed to ignore it. If

it gets out of hand I simply hit *snooze, mute,* or *unfollow*. People want to say what they want to say. I don't have to butt-in or take offense all the time. We control what constantly shows up in our feeds by what we continually interact with. Nobody else does. So if our feeds and stories are splatter-blasters of crap, fear-mongering, and hate; if, once a month we post, "I'm done! I can't stand what I see on social media any longer!" *we* have the power to change that. Keep scrolling away from that stuff and don't engage with it. Begin interacting with gentle and respectful people, groups, and pages! Your social media experience will change for the better!

A prayer for you: *Heavenly Father, how amazing are the ideas you've given us for technology! The internet is allowing us to learn and grow on unprecedented levels! The days of needing to go stand in front of someone once or twice a week to hear their opinion about you is being exceeded from our own pockets! But at the same time, this technology can be hurtful and frustrating when we don't let your Spirit work through it. Continue to teach us how to use what you've given us to express you properly. Right now, I lift up all who are reading this, directly to you. Help them to grow in your grace and to be able to get their point across kindly. If there's constant turmoil with their social media, let them know they have the capability to change this themselves. Teach us all how to spread the Good News without being combative. We want the world to see you through us. You are loving, patient, kind, gentle, and respectful. Amen.*

Day 16

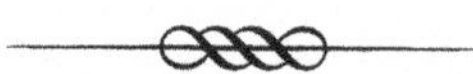

Can Christians Lose Fellowship With God?

"For I am convinced that neither death nor life, neither angels nor demons, neither the present nor the future, nor any powers, neither height nor depth, nor anything else in all creation, will be able to separate us from the love of God that is in Christ Jesus our Lord."

Romans 8:38-39

The short answer is, "No, we cannot lose fellowship with God."

I'd even say this: The phrasing of the question is wrong because fellowship and relationship, with God, is the same thing.

I used this particular query as the title of this devotional because it's used so often by those who chop up our union with God into sections based on our actions and attitudes. If we look into Scripture, the word *fellowship* is used approximately ten times in the New Testament, but not once is the context referring to a Christian receiving the silent treatment from God for sinning.

Am I pro-sin? Of course not. When we sin it's only smart to stop. Sinning is bad for us and others. As children of God we've been recreated in spirit to no *longer* sin. Paul said we've died to it; he said Christ is not promoting sin just because He's justified us (see Romans 6:2-11, Galatians 2:17).

Therefore *when* we sin, we should turn from it every time but never to receive more forgiveness, and never to get back into fellowship with God.

THE CROSS ACHIEVED ABSOLUTE FELLOWSHIP FOR ALL WHO'S EVER BELIEVED, ONCE AND FOR ALL TIME (see John 17:23, 1 Corinthians 1:9).

Unlike human relationships, with God, only blood forgives and nothing else. The author of Hebrews tells us without the shedding of blood there is no forgiveness (see Hebrews 9:22). Why do you think Jesus had to die a *bloody* death and not some other way, such as hanging?

Blood had to be shed.

Continual repenting doesn't continually forgive us either, it's not blood. But even if it did, how could we be sure we repented well enough? The legalist will tell you, but they aren't believing in *only* Christ's blood, instead, their own works. This group will be turned away at heaven (see Matthew 7:21-23, Romans 11:6).

Continual confessing doesn't continually forgive us either, it's not blood. But even if it did, how could we be sure we remembered every single sin? God doesn't forget just because we forget. And why don't we just go ahead and do a lifetime blanket confession? Or why not just *overlook* sins and attempt to justify them with excuses? And what about the sins we forget to confess?

A person who struggles with religious tendencies will scream, "Those are *willful* sins, Matt! Only willful sins count!"

Well they can raise their voice all they like, the reality is, our wills are involved every time we sin. All sins are willful. There's no such thing as an accidental sin. According to the Law of Moses? Yes, because there were 613 sins to remember, but not now. We don't get to pick stuff out from the Law for our liking, it's all or nothing (see Deuteronomy 4:2, James 2:10, Galatians 3:10, Ephesians 2:12-19).

Since Jesus came and brought in the New Covenant, therefore setting aside the first Covenant made by Moses, the Bible says anything that is not of faith is sin. Good luck trying to cherry-pick sins, both for yourself and for others (see Luke 22:20, Romans 14:23, Hebrews 10:9).

The "continue to sin willfully" passage from Hebrews 10:26 is referring to Jews sinning according to the Law. This doesn't apply to Christians because we aren't trying to receive forgiveness from animal blood at the temple—they were. The Law required it. *That* was the problem. They were willfully sinning according to the Old Covenant, the Law. Are we doing this? No, friends, we are not. We've died to the Law in full so that we can live for Christ! All laws! Self-made, church-made, or Mosaic! (See Galatians 2:19, 5:1, Romans 7:4).

Simply read down to verse 29 in Hebrews chapter 10 to see the full context of the *continue to sin willfully* threat. It's sinning according to Moses, not Jesus, so stop worrying about being forgiven for willful sins. I REPEAT: STOP WORRYING ABOUT SINNING.

If you sin, Christian, you are *already* forgiven (see James 5:15). God knows you'll sin but He's decided to not hold it against you (see Hebrews 8:12). The sooner you understand this, the sooner you'll sin less because "stopping sinning" won't be your focus. Living righteously will because that's what you are! (See 1 Corinthians 1:30, 6:11, 2 Corinthians 5:21, 1 John 2:29, Romans 6:18).

The next question is, does our good works cause us to get back into fellowship with God? No way. Our best works are like filthy rags apart from

Christ (see Isaiah 64:6, Ephesians 2:8-9, John 15:5). As I mentioned in the opening, some claim we can lose fellowship with God but not our relationship. They preach we must do good works, confess sins, and cut back on sinning to achieve fellowship over and over, yet they claim our *relationship* is secure.

This is worse than Old Testament Judaism, as even they didn't chop up fellowship and relationship based on works, confession, and less sinning. Animal bloodshed once a year at the Day of Atonement gave them a clear conscience for another 365 days worth of sinning. They knew nothing could be done about their sins—transgressions of the Law—until blood was offered up the following year. As a result, the Hebrew people never worried about fellowship nor relationship being broken; an annual animal slaughter took care of both.

Sore thumbs galore stick out in a person's theology when we mention the truth which overrides the list of things they claim we must do repeatedly to get back into fellowship: *Jesus' blood forgave us forever, even of future sins.*

Their heads spin, they can't compute, and here's what they can't fathom:

ALL OUR SINS WERE IN THE FUTURE WHEN CHRIST DIED FOR THEM.

Think about it, we get our very notion of time from the sun and planets in which He created. Who are we to say He can't forgive the future? He can! He does! He did! For all who will believe in Him once! Remember, only blood forgives. Christ isn't getting up and down on a cross in heaven each time we sin.

IT. IS. FINISHED.

The author of Hebrews is adamant, God forgives every sin for every believer once and for all time by one offering, the bloody body of Jesus! (See Hebrews 1:3, 7:27, 10:1-18). The wages of sin is a bloody death, not God sticking His fingers in His ears. JESUS CHRIST DIED (see Romans 6:23). So we have to come up with a better reason to change our sinful actions and attitudes rather than repeated forgiveness or trying to get back into fellowship. How about we make healthy changes because God wants the best for us like a good father does? This only makes sense.

Lastly, some will use 1 John 1 as the go-to chapter to prove we *can* lose fellowship with God for sinning. But upon further review, the only way we can come to such a conclusion is when we don't understand two things:

1. The first chapter of 1 John is an invitation to unbelievers to join believers in fellowship with God through faith in Christ's ability to forgive them *once*. That's why it says they'll be cleansed of *all* unrighteousness. All means all. We can't lose fellowship if we are perfectly cleansed because only sin can separate us from God—yet we've been cleansed. Believers are then addressed in the beginning of chapter 2. The first chapter isn't directed at us. We can read it, but context matters tremendously.
2. Confession, just like repentance, is normal and healthy for Christians; however, neither keep God pleased with us, saved, forgiven, or in fellowship. Only Jesus' life, bloody death, and resurrection does that and our entering *into* Him by faith, once. Jesus will always stay alive. He will always stay faithful. So we will always stay pleasing to God, saved, forgiven, and in fellowship (see John 1:12-13, 14:9, Hebrews 4:11, 7:24-25, 12:2, 1 John 2:2, 2 Corinthians 2:15, 5:21).

So today, my friends, know this: God never turns away from us! God never removes fellowship until we "shape up"! He's our doting Dad! Be confident in His love for you! The Cross was a huge success and you're God's masterpiece!

A prayer for you: *Father, recently a lady said to me, "You mean to tell me, if I don't take time to talk to God for two or three days in a row, and I ignore Him, you think I still have fellowship with Him!?" I didn't answer her because she was already worked up into a hateful lather, but yes, absolutely! If the world only knew how secure you are in being our Father, they'd never see you in such a pouty, immature view! Right now, I lift up all who are reading this, directly to you. For the believers, remind them they are one with you. We can't get more fellowshippy than that! For the unbelievers, keep speaking to them, Dad. Keep letting them know how much you love them. Help their unbelief. In Christ's name I pray, amen.*

Day 17

Did God Send the Coronavirus to Humble the World?

"If my people who are called by my name will humble themselves and pray and seek my face and turn from their wicked ways, then I will hear from heaven and will forgive their sin and will heal their land."

2 Chronicles 7:14

When the virus first hit, there was a cluster of lies circulating in a Facebook post about COVID-19. Someone was blaming God for the Coronavirus.

Here's the post:

In three short months, just like He did with the plagues of Egypt, God has taken away everything we worship. God said, "You want to worship athletes, I will shut down the stadiums. You want to worship musicians, I will shut down Civic Centers. You want to worship actors, I will shut down theaters. You want to worship money, I will shut down the economy and collapse the stock market. You don't want to go to church and worship Me, I will make it where you can't go to church."

"If my people who are called by my name will humble themselves and pray and seek my face and turn from their wicked ways, then I will hear from heaven and will forgive their sin and will heal their land." (2 Chronicles 7:14)

Maybe we don't need a vaccine. Maybe we need to take this time of isolation from the distractions of the world and have a personal revival where we focus on the ONLY thing in the world that really matters. Jesus.

Here are the lies:

1. **The entire first paragraph is not in the Bible.** It's made up by someone who wants to put words in God's mouth to make their own legalistic points. It belittles the Cross and makes God seem as if the blood of Jesus didn't fully work for Him; as if He's still mad and Christ didn't finish *anything* for us. (See John 19:30, Hebrews 1:3, 9:22, 10:10, 1 John 2:2)
2. **God does not send plagues to "take away" athletes, stadiums, musicians, Civic Centers, actors, theaters, money, nor does He collapse the stock market.** That would mean He is also taking away schools, churches, charities, missions, and other *good* things as this virus shut down *all* gatherings. God is not vindictive, but loving and kind, no longer dealing with humanity on the basis of sins. Why? Because of the Cross. (See Galatians 5:22-23, 1 Corinthians 13:4-8, Hebrews 9:28, John 1:29)

3. **The Bible verse from 2 Chronicles 7:14 was written to the *old* nation of Israel, not America—and not even the current State of Israel.** This passage is thousands of years old. America was established in the summer of 1776, and Israel, May 14, 1948. This passage does not apply to us. Instead, it's directed at the Jewish people group who rebelled against God and the Law of Moses. We Americans can *know* this passage, but it's not our mail. Context is key. (See Deuteronomy 4:2, 5:2, Ephesians 2:12)
4. **The last paragraph says we need a "personal revival" and I fell for this lie for years.** We don't need a revival but our minds renewed to the truth of what Christ has done *for* us and *to* us. Revival means "to relive" or "to come back to life," BUT THIS HAS ALREADY HAPPENED FOR CHRISTIANS! What do you think occurred the moment we believed in Jesus? We died on the Cross *with* Him, we were buried in the tomb *with* Him, and came back to life—WITH HIM! WE DON'T NEED TO KEEP COMING BACK TO LIFE, WE NEED TO LIVE! (See Romans 6:6-10, 12:2, Galatians 2:20, Colossians 3:3-4, 1 Corinthians 6:17, 2 Corinthians 5:17,21)

Here are these lies deciphered in view of the Cross:

1. **On this side of the Cross, God does not send plagues. HE IS FOR US, NOT AGAINST US.** He sent plagues to Egypt to protect the line of Judah, which came from Israel, in order to protect the lineage of the Messiah, Jesus. After these plagues were sent and Pharaoh released the Hebrew people, God made a Covenant with *them* through *Moses* at Mount Sinai. He was the mediator of the Old Covenant, Jesus is the Mediator of the New Covenant. It was there, at Sinai, the Law was put into place (the Old Covenant). At the Cross, the New replaced the Old,

as only one Covenant can be in effect at a time. When Christ came and died a *new* Covenant replaced the one which came through Moses—the Law—FOR ALL WHO WILL BELIEVE IN HIM. This Covenant happened at the death of Jesus, not His birth, because only blood can bring in a new Covenant and only a perfect Priest can present such blood to God. Jesus did this ONCE unlike the now obsolete priests from the tribe of Levi who presented blood over and over (*side note* all of today's priests are obsolete as well; fake middlemen, mere humans attempting to replace Jesus as Mediator. They aren't Jewish. They aren't from Levi. The temple is gone. The Messiah replaced them). The bottom line is, everything Israel—and all of humanity—would ever do, say, or think *sinfully*, it was placed on the Cross. Blame Jesus, not me. (See Mark 2:22, Hebrews 3:1-6, all of Hebrews 7, 8:6-13, 9:12-25, 10:10, John 1:17, Romans 8:28-31, 10:14, 1 Timothy 2:5)

2. **If God sent the Coronavirus to take everything away from us "to teach us a lesson" then the Cross wasn't good enough for Him.** It would be weak and useless. The truth is, HE DID NOT SEND THIS HERE. We live in a fallen world with death and decay. *We* did this, Adam and Eve, not God. He created everything perfect including us. *We* messed this place up. Not Him. HE CREATED THIS PLANET "AND IT WAS GOOD." Instead, He knew this would happen and devised a rescue mission before Creation. Jesus. Through Him, by grace through faith, His Spirit comforts us during stressful times. He isn't "sending plagues" on one side of us and then scurrying around to the other side to comfort us. He's not a psycho. Legalistic people may do this but not God. He's a good Father, and good fathers would never hand their child a stone when they ask for bread. (See Genesis chapters 1-3, Romans 5:1-9, Revelation 13:8, John 14:26, Matthew 7:9, Ephesians 2:8-9)

3. **2 Chronicles 7:14 is directed at the Jewish people who rebelled against the Law of Moses.** They had promised God through Moses, they would do *everything* written in the Book of the Law—all 613 commandments, not just 10 like we hand-pick today. This was *before* the Cross, according to the *Old* Covenant, and it's a threat to *that* group whom Moses had led out of Egypt. The temple had just been built and Solomon was dedicating it with thousands of cattle being slaughtered for their blood. On *this* side of the Cross, through *Jesus'* blood, Israel was taken *out* of the Covenant and a *new* Covenant was made. Jesus was inserted into *their* place *and* ours, we Gentiles (anyone who isn't Jewish). Now, the Covenant is based on a promise between God and God—Father and Son (who cannot lie, like Israel, or you and me)—the Old Covenant was finished at the Cross. In lieu of Calvary, instead of humanity being "promise keepers" (like Israel before the Cross), we've become beneficiaries to *their* promise to *one another*. Beneficiaries do nothing except *receive* by way of a death. Jesus died. Therefore, we can't apply this verse to us about the virus. God no longer sends plagues, He sent Jesus. Christ was enough. (See Exodus 19:8, John 19:30, James 2:10, Galatians 3:10,18,28, Hebrews 6:16-19, Ephesians 1:7-14, 2 Timothy 2:13)
4. **The last paragraph is just some good old-fashioned Christian guilt—which never works. It creates stress or hypocrisy, neither of which are from God.** (See Matthew 15:7-9, 11:28-30, Hebrews 4:11, Acts 20:24, Romans 11:6)

I do, however, agree with the part which says, "The only thing that matters is Jesus." So if the only thing that matters is Jesus, let's stop lying about what He's fully done for us at the Cross. That event was a huge success!

So today, my friends, know this: God's wrath over the sin of humanity was satisfied! He is comforting those who have believed and wooing those who have not (see Romans 2:4, 5:1,9). He's now working in us and through us at all times, especially during trying seasons. Express Him, love others, be easy on yourself and be confident.

A prayer for you: *Heavenly Father, you are so good to us. I hope more people come to understand this truth. If only the world knew how satisfied you are because of Jesus, they'd change their attitudes about you. They'd stop flinching and begging and they'd start thanking and praising. Right now, I lift up all who are reading this, directly to you. Dad, please open up their minds to the truth of the gospel. Reveal what Christ has done! Help them to begin to see Him as He truly is, which in turn will help them begin to see your goodness. In His name I pray, amen.*

Day 18

Are You a Victim of Trauma?

"It is not the healthy who need a doctor, but the sick." ~Jesus

See Matthew 9:12

Trauma can impact our lives negatively, in so many ways, especially if we don't take steps to heal from it. First, let's define trauma: *a deeply distressing or disturbing experience.*

Here are ten examples:

1. **Molestation** – What was done to you was not okay. That relative, neighbor, or person was wrong—VERY WRONG. This was not your fault.
2. **Abandonment** – That parent, spouse, friend, or loved one left because of their own issues, not because of you. This was not your fault.
3. **War** – The excruciating things you've seen and experienced were part of your everyday life as you simply did your job. Just because you're

back home physically doesn't mean you're back mentally. You were in survival mode for so long and now you don't know how to *not* be in survival mode. This is not your fault.

4. **Religion** – God's character is nothing like the people who treated you like trash. That manipulation didn't come from Him, even if they acted like it did. He loves you. He's always gentle, patient, and kind toward you, even while correcting you. This was not your fault.
5. **Physical injury** – It's a tragedy what happened to you and there's nothing that can be done to change it. But this isn't the end of your life. God can still bring you great joy and purpose, even through your adversity—if not more.
6. **The silent treatment** – This can be considered a type of abandonment only it's repeated again and again, sometimes over the course of a lifetime. They shut you out and it hurts. As a result, you overlook your own well-being and needs, scrambling to please them, but it doesn't work. Even if it does, it's normally not good enough or doesn't last long; that is, until they give you the cold shoulder yet again. Thankfully, God never does such a traumatic thing to you. This is that *person's* bag of crap, not yours. Let them hold on to it while you enjoy your life. Not your fault.
7. **Adultery** – Physical and emotional adultery is rampant today due to social media. There's never been an easier way to be cheated on. You can be sleeping in one room and your spouse is cheating in the other. This isn't your fault no matter what they say or excuses they give, especially when you catch them. If you haven't caught them yet, you will, *if* they're doing this to you.
8. **Public dishonor** – Reputations are ruined with the stroke of some keys, every day. Used to be, when you broke up with someone only a handful of people knew about it. Now the status of *Single, Separated,*

Divorced, or whatever is front page news on everyone's feed. But it doesn't stop there. Lazy and dishonest employees who were fired, former friends who did you wrong, and even salty relatives can put stuff online as if it's true. Public dishonor is *so* prevalent for teens, their suicide rate is at an all-time high. This trauma isn't your fault.

9. **Death of a loved one** – The loss of a child is unimaginable; the passing of someone in the prime of their life or even while *struggling* with life, this is a devastating trauma. Of course, not your fault.
10. **Divorce** – The severing of a family impacts so many different people on so many different levels, not just the two divorcing. The destructive domino effect for the children and generations to come, along with the gut-wrenching emotions caused by this trauma? *Astronomical.*

Friend, I understand there are many more types of trauma. I'm so sorry you've experienced such anguish. It wasn't fair and your feelings are valid and important. *You* are important. Your life is important. If I've missed your trauma, fill in the blank:

"_________________________ is my trauma. This was not my fault."

Unfortunately, serious issues can develop from trauma:

Knee-jerk bitter reactions (even toward those who truly care for us), extreme distrust, debilitating fear, social anxiety, private anxiety, constant worry, sleeplessness, night terrors, hair-trigger anger, alcoholism, drug addiction, food addiction, sex addiction, porn addiction, gambling addiction, electronics addiction, isolation, workaholism, rage, working out excessively, indulging in hobbies excessively, extreme laziness, depression, sweeping the issues of others under the rug, codependency, people-pleasing, pastoral worship, pastoral hate, church worship, church hate, denying sex for your spouse, using sex as a bartering tool, projecting, gas lighting, legalism, licentiousness, placating, lack of boundaries, lack of time management, and more.

How to heal from trauma:

1. **Feel your feelings** – "It's so messed up you feel that way!" is a lie coming from someone who doesn't understand just how important your feelings are. You *must* feel your feelings and *not* ignore them. God gave you the ability to feel for a reason. Feelings aren't right or wrong, they're indicators of what's happening *to* you, *around* you, and in your mind. Feel what you need to feel and don't feel bad about it. If you *do* feel bad about it, let yourself feel bad, then move forward knowing *that* feeling is fine too. Let yourself *feeeeeeeeel*! Rule of thumb: Don't let your feelings lead you, let God lead you, but never think that God is telling you *not* to feel. He wants to guide you *as* you feel. Big difference.
2. **Hold the person responsible who caused you trauma** – This is hard. It's hard because we can take this to the extreme either way; blaming them for everything—for *every* problem in our life—or *never* holding them responsible for anything. Don't do either. Instead, make a decision to say, "Your choices caused me severe pain, this is why: ____________________. You owed me ____________________. It's not okay you didn't give this to me. You hurt me greatly and have impacted my life negatively." Even if they aren't there to hear you, have passed away, or if they never hear this, say it so *you* can hear it. If it's the government, war enemy, or even God, you can still do the same thing. For God, you won't hurt His feelings. He understands your

pain even though He didn't cause it. He's secure, so express yourself! Cast all your anxieties on Him because He cares!

3. **Choose to forgive** – Jesus understood the foundation of true peace and fulfillment: *forgive those who have hurt you.* The legalist will say, "If you don't forgive others God won't forgive you!" but that's a lie which causes *more* trauma. Jesus said this to the Mosaic Law-lovers to get them to turn toward faith in Him alone. Those self-righteous jerks thought they could forgive their way to heaven and Jesus was pointing out their failures. On this side of the Cross we forgive to release ourselves from another's grasp on our soul, never to *be* forgiven. The person who's harmed you doesn't even have to know you've forgiven them, but they can, if you want to tell them. You don't have to feel like forgiving or wait until you're ready, nor is forgiveness a process. *Trust* is a process, yes, but forgiveness is an instant choice of our will. Simply say, "At this time, on this date, I choose to release you from what you owe me," and then watch what God does with your attitude.
4. **Establish boundaries** – Healthy boundaries are always founded on love, both for yourself and the other person. Boundaries aren't walls, they are see-through fences with gates meant to protect you and others. The gates let people in, show people out, and also allow us to take out our own trash. Boundaries determine where *we* begin and *others* end; our responsibilities and theirs. Boundaries allow self-care and create clear minds. Boundaries teach us to not be so hard on ourselves and to notice when others are. Boundaries say, "No." "Not now." "Sure." "That won't work for me." "I've changed my mind." "This needs to change because I care." "I love you, but that's not okay." Boundaries are calm. Boundaries are not reactive. Boundaries are our responsibility, not anyone else's. Boundaries allow us to think about the worst

possible outcome and remain peaceful, even in the midst of the pain. Anger is the baby steps of boundaries, serenity is the maturation. Boundaries are not ultimatums but loving and respectful cornerstones of relational life. I recommend the book series *Boundaries,* by Henry Cloud and John Townsend, to everyone who's experienced trauma.

5. **Grow in God's grace** – The Bible says the grace of God teaches us how to live our lives! (See Titus 2:11-12). Grace is not an add-on to stuff; grace-based this, grace-based that. Grace is our very life! Grace is Jesus and Jesus is grace! So grow in grace and grow in Him! He's the true Healer of every trauma we've ever had or ever will!

A prayer for you: *Father, thank you so much for helping me heal from my past traumas and continuing to do so. Thank you for always being there for me when others weren't, and even when I wasn't kind to myself. Thank you for guiding me toward the truth of your great love, and teaching me there's nothing wrong with me. I'm forever grateful for your Spirit within. Right now, I lift up all who are reading this, directly to you. Countless people are suffering, Dad. The trauma they've experienced, or still are, isn't fair. Encourage them to feel their feelings and to fall into you for advice, guidance, wisdom, and comfort. You use all things together for good. You make everything new, including our mindsets. Thank you. In Christ's name, amen.*

Day 19

Heart to Head, Not Head to Heart

"Do not let your hearts be troubled and do not be afraid." ~Jesus

See John 14:27

We've got it backwards. We've been told to never follow our hearts because they're wicked and deceitful. We *think* we can't let our *hearts* lead us and that our *heads* must do the job. Countless Christians don't know what happened at the Cross, as a result, multitudes will claim, "I believe it in my head, now I just have to believe it in my heart."

We think head-to-heart, not heart-to-head, but that's backwards. This is a big deal because we're overlooking our identity as suffice for making choices.

As children of God we *want* our hearts to lead our heads—our thoughts and attitudes—because we have *good* hearts, hearts like God. Our hearts have been made new. The Spirit of Jesus Christ lives there permanently. He's not coming and going based on our actions and mindsets.

From your heart, He wants to renew your mind, not the other way around. Your heart is final, it is your *mind* being renewed over the course of your brief lifetime (see Romans 12:2, Philippians 4:8). How can I make such a claim? Because Christians have been given new spiritual hearts!

The Covenant-mixing theologian will be furious, "You're wrong, Matt! We have wicked, sinful, deceitful hearts!"

No friend, that is what we *had*. That is what we *were*. But we were washed, we were justified, we were sanctified from the millisecond of believing, *Jesus has forgiven me? Wow, Jesus has forgiven me!* (See 1 Corinthians 6:11, John 1:12-13, 3:16-18).

Before this belief in the Son of God? Yes, absolutely, we had wicked, sinful, deceitful hearts, but that was *before* salvation. What do you think happened to you when you first believed on Jesus? A partial cleaning? Never. Such would require Christ to die again and again because only blood can cleanse. Here's the truth, believer:

YOU'VE BEEN REMADE AS A NEW, SPOTLESS, COMPLETE CREATION.
(See 2 Corinthians 5:17, Colossians 1:22, 2:9-10)

Therefore, all the Bible verses about wicked, sinful, deceitful hearts, do not apply to you—your identity. Context matters when reading this stuff. Sure, we might have some unrenewed, immature *thoughts*, but we are not our thoughts—good, bad, or indifferent. Instead, our *heart* is working on those *with* the Counselor of Christ within us. He is who reminds us of everything (see John 14:26).

Further, the majority of the "bad heart," "guard my heart," "who can know the heart" passages were before the Cross. Those Hebrew people longed for what we now have on this side of Golgotha (see Hebrews 11). If they had the opportunity *to* believe in the Messiah—which they did not—they knew exactly what He'd do to their sinful hearts. He'd replace them.

One of their Prophets, Ezekiel, explained what God would do to their hearts, hundreds of years before Jesus came to earth:

> *"I will give you a new heart and put a new spirit in you; I will remove from you your heart of stone and give you a heart of flesh."*
> *(Ezekiel 36:26)*

New hearts, new spirits—soft like flesh, which is the opposite of hard stone.

God cannot live in wicked, sinful places, so He killed you—your heart, your spirit—then He recreated you as new. *Then* He moved in, and not a moment sooner (see Galatians 2:20, 1 Corinthians 6:19, John 14:23, 17:23). How do you think Jesus' Spirit *can* live in you? It's only because your spirit is sinless. Your spirit only became sinless because it died on the Cross, was buried in the tomb, and then resurrected as new (see Romans 6:3-11).

Since Jesus *physically* came and went, only those who *refuse* His offer of new life have unregenerate, sinful hearts. Not you, dear believer. You've died, came back to life, and now you're hidden *in* Christ. You are one with Jesus' Holy Spirit (see Colossians 3:3, 1 Corinthians 6:17, Romans 8:9).

You can now live from the heart, give from the heart, set boundaries from the heart, be confident from the heart, work from the heart, love your spouse from the heart, parent your kids from the heart, enjoy your hobbies from the heart—*express* yourself—*from the heart.*

You have a good heart, a sinless heart, a complete heart, a special heart. You literally want what God wants, from the heart, by way of your new, godly, divine nature (see Romans 6:17, 2 Corinthians 9:6-8, Colossians 2:9-10, 2 Peter 1:4).

You lack *nothing*... from the heart.

So today, my friends, know this: Let your heart lead your head, not the other way around. Renew your mind from who you are inside. Always follow your heart! Let your head catch *up* to your amazing heart! Let God within you reshape and mature your thinking! *Think* different because you *are* different, from the heart!

A prayer for you: *Father, today I want to express my appreciation to you for teaching me the truth about my heart. For too many years I believed I had a wicked, sinful heart, and the enemy loved this. He loved this because he knows we will live out who we believe we are. "You're wicked anyway, so just act wicked! It's who you are, Matt!" this moron would say this to me. Now that I know what you've done to my identity, my heart, he stands no chance. I hardly pay any attention to him anymore. Instead, I pay attention to who I am! Right now, I lift up all who are reading this, directly to you. Dad, please renew their minds to what you've done to their hearts, for those who have believed. It just makes sense! You've recreated them! They're not guarding their hearts, that was before the Cross; they are now EXPRESSING their hearts! It is your PEACE which is now guarding their hearts—not them! Keep counseling these dear people into their amazing regenerated identity. In Christ's name, amen.*

Day 20

Diary of a Former Closet Drinker

"Behold, God is my helper; the Lord is the sustainer of my soul."

Psalm 54:4

I've titled this devotional *Diary of a Former Closet Drinker* but let's be clear about something. I, my identity, was never "closet drinker." Instead, that's what I struggled with. I only have so much space in the box to enter a title, so that's what I went with. But I am not what I do—good, bad, or indifferent. I'm an unchangeable, complete *saint*. God did this not me. He recreated my spirit like Jesus' the millisecond of my salvation. You, dear Christian, are a saint too. There aren't different levels of sainthood. We are all the same; equal in identity.

Let's continue.

For those of us who've chosen to no longer act on what we were addicted to—for me, namely binge drinking—we count the days of sobriety at first. No, scratch that. We count the *hours*.

My addiction always flared up the worst after work each day and on Friday evenings. Even though I battled passing up the liquor store on my way home, I never woke up in the middle of the night reaching out for a whiskey bottle in an attempt to stop shaking. This was one of my best excuses.

"Ain't nobody stopping me from having an ice-cold beer and a few shots! I'm not like those bad alcoholics! I know how to control it! Don't compare me to them!"

Belittling and deflecting was my specialty when it came to discussing my severe drinking problem. I would even become defensive when *other* people's alcohol addiction was being discussed and I wasn't even the topic.

"Oh yeah, they're *real* bad. For me, I just buy what I'm going to drink and be done. I can't be getting drunk all the time."

Ha! Yeah right. I could sneak-drink with the best of them; closet drinking is what some call it. When all the normal drinkers were just getting started, I had already smashed two tall-boys and three shots. Pre-gaming it, privately. If my wife and I were getting ready to go somewhere, I'd sneak-drink half a bottle of her wine in a plastic cup—unbeknownst to her—or so I thought. Jennifer knew. She wasn't stupid. She would be hurt and frustrated, but I could manipulate her with sweet words or self-pity. Because she's so kind and sensitive, I took advantage of that.

When I really got on a roll of "too many days of hangovers," to prove I wasn't that bad of a drinker I'd take a day or two off and not touch anything. To prove I'm *really* no lush I'd even go a week! No matter though. I wasn't fooling myself, even when lying to myself. I knew as soon as I got back to "enjoying" beers and shots, my off-button would still be broken.

I tried this charade a thousand times. Honestly, if I do the math, more than that.

I also used humor to take the focus off my inability to give it up. Eventually anger toward myself and depression darkened my days. I *wanted it* though.

I *wanted* to give it up. No amount of codependent enabling from our loved ones will ever make us stop. *We* have to come to the point of realizing those who coddle us are wrong too. They may very well be addicted to us being addicted, and just don't know it.

After nearly six years in recovery, I *know* what I've truly recovered from:

Not being comfortable in my own skin.

Now I am, and I have been for quite some time.

There's a release we get in our mind and body when the buzz begins. It's an exhale, not from our lungs, but from our thoughts, *Aaaaahhhh... there it is...* We feel it. We let our eyes close and whisper to ourselves, "I wish I could feel this 24/7."

Miller Lite and American Honey was what I mainly used, but I'll take whatever craft beer you have and some Patron—or Jameson, or both. Whatever. Just give it to me. I'll drink your wine too when I'm out of beer or when I'm trying to appear cultured.

Mixed drinks? I mostly stayed away from those because I don't know how to sip anything and I'll get absolutely trashed—quickly. Be that as it may, I'll have those too if need be.

The person who struggles with heroin chooses to use a small amount of liquid opioid and a needle. I had a frosty bottle and a small shot-glass. Our actions were no different only our vices. Although you won't see any billboards or TV commercials to shoot up heroin, alcohol destroys lives just the same, but it's sexy and legal.

Don't get me wrong, alcohol isn't bad. It can't drink itself or force itself into stomachs. And not everyone has a sinful tendency to get obliterated like me. Many can enjoy it, have a few, and be done. Jesus was a great example. I could never seem to pull this off with any true consistency. I tried for many years. Attempting to control and enjoy my drinking became an obsession. Never could I combine those two words:

Control. Enjoy.
Enjoy. Control.

It was like trying to push the polar sides of magnets together. Nope.

"You people are weak!" someone might say. "You should be able to stop anytime you want!" As they watch their porn, cheat on their spouse emotionally, overeat, smoke, and/or strive to follow the Law of Moses, they're blind to their own addictions. It took me years to understand these hypocritical facts.

God has taught me *anyone* can choose to act on *anything* to give them a temporary release—a *feeling* of peace. What most of us don't understand is that the Holy Spirit has the market cornered on this release—on this peaceful feeling. No, He's not altering our feelings or giving us a buzz at our request. Rather, He generously supplies a tranquil foundation to recenter our feelings onto:

Identity.

He encourages *all* feelings whereas alcohol abuse doesn't. Feelings are not sin. Acting on certain feelings *can* be, but the feeling in itself is neutral and we must know this. Drinking *heavily* numbs what we *need* to feel; it dulls that which is essential to expressing ourselves in healthy ways with *fake* feelings. Alcohol in excess hands us a faux euphoria we'll have to chase again, and again, and again ...

It's nearly demonic. I'll not go as far as saying we're being demonically accused each and every episode of binge drinking, but I know the demons I screamed at during my darkest hours of late-night drunkenness. I remember the nightmares and the night terrors. Sobriety has ended this completely.

The Spirit doesn't want us to mask our emotions caused by trauma, stress, pressure, fear, failure, and anxiety. He encourages us to feel whatever we feel, to not feel bad about feeling, and then to look to Him for truth and peace about whatever we feel.

So today, my friends, know this: Feel, friend. Feel. Feel. Feel. Never stop feeling. You are loved.

A prayer for you: *Dad, good morning. It's a cold, wet, dark day here in the Show-Me State. Yet I know that even when the day is drab you are my bright warm light on the inside. I'm safe and secure. Right now, I lift up all who are reading this, directly to you. Some who were enjoying sobriety have relapsed. Let them know you're still with them and you've never left. Remind them that you know how they feel and you'll comfort them. Strengthen them, Father, please. Encourage them to feel whatever they feel and to free-fall into your grace for sufficiency. We love you. We're grateful for you. Amen.*

Day 21

Was Judas Saved?

"Then one of the Twelve, the one called Judas Iscariot, went to the chief priests"

Matthew 26:14

It's shocking to me how we like to decide who's saved and who *isn't* saved based on someone's actions, attitudes, and outward appearances. We, created beings, have the tendency to determine the salvation of an individual in lieu of a life of church work and servitude, or habitual wrongdoing and that "big" sin.

Paul warned the Romans about doing this when he wrote, "Don't say who will ascend or descend; if you've believed in Jesus you will be saved" (see Romans 10:6-9). Yet so many of the "committed" don't like this. They want to be God. Those words won't come out of their mouths, but they judge others and determine people's salvation by way of their own opinion on top of a semi-grace interpretation of specific biblical passages.

Nobody has ever been more judged in human history, in regard to their eternal security, than Judas Iscariot. Hitler, maybe? But Judas had a 1,900-year head start.

Judas is also the poster boy for the legalist to hang up on their wall, point to and say, "Look! Judas is proof you can lose your salvation!"

Why though? Why do we get to make this determination? Is it because he betrayed Jesus? Does Christ no longer keep saved those who betray Him in word and deed? I don't see that anywhere in Scripture. In fact, I see the opposite.

For a long time, I personally said, "No, Judas was *not* saved," but I've had to repent of this notion. Who am *I* to say whether or not he was saved? Who am I to make this claim? I'm clay. I'm not the Potter. The reality is, had I been there on the night Jesus was arrested I could very well be the one who forsook Him with a kiss.

I am a human being. Fallible. So was Judas.

"Wrong, Matt! Judas was chosen by God *for* that role! He was hand-selected to be damned to hell!"

So is God now choosing to damn people to hell before they're created? Where's the free will involved with such a theology? I thought God's desire is that nobody should perish? (See 2 Peter 3:9). Judas doesn't count?

Just because God can see the future doesn't mean He's controlling those whom He's created. He's not bound by time, we are (see 2 Peter 3:8).

For many years I thought Judas wasn't a Christian because both Luke *and* John said Satan entered him (see Luke 22:3, John 13:2). However, keep in mind, this was before Pentecost so the enemy still had this right. After Pentecost, the permanent indwelling of the Holy Spirit would never allow any demonic force to enter a child of God again. We are sealed up forever protected by Him! (See Ephesians 1:13, 1 John 5:18).

Some will say Christ Himself announced that Judas was doomed, based on John 17:12, "He's the son of perdition, Matt! Judas was fated for destruction!"

But I don't think it's so cut and dry. Pay close attention to what I've underlined:

> *"While I was with them, I kept them in your name, which you have given me. I have guarded them, and not one of them has been lost except the son of destruction, that the Scripture might be fulfilled."*
> *(John 17:12)*

This simply says he was lost from the group of disciples, not from Christ. In context, that's who Jesus is praying for. Why did Judas drop out? So Scripture would be fulfilled. It doesn't say he *didn't* get saved at some point. And what is the destruction? Is it him or is it what he did? Messiah doesn't say. It's not there so we can't assume. My opinion is this: *we should lean toward grace and the love of God in such a situation.* Also, if you want to say Acts 1 proves he's in hell, that's not true either. I go over that passage in the prayer at the end of this devotional.

What most promise keepers won't focus on is *after* Judas conducted the most diabolical backstabbing in history, he repented, or at least it appeared that way according to Matthew:

> *Then when Judas, his betrayer, saw that Jesus was condemned, he changed his mind and brought back the thirty pieces of silver to the chief priests and the elders, saying, "I have sinned by betraying innocent blood." (See Matthew 27:3-4)*

He repented. He changed his mind. He claimed Jesus was innocent and that he was a sinner. Is this not enough to be saved?

The person who's fixated on how well-behaved they are will shout, "It's clear, Matt! Read your Bible! Jesus even said woe to the one who betrays the Son of Man! It would be better if they weren't even born!" (See Matthew 26:24).

But friend, is that not you? Is that not me? Have we not *all* betrayed Him? Yes, we have.

Lastly, in his great turmoil, Judas killed himself. Why would his desertion of Jesus bother him to the point of suicide if he *wasn't* saved? Wouldn't you think he'd be celebrating with Satan instead of dealing with such guilt?

Some believe that killing yourself is unforgivable, but that's not true. We aren't saved by our ability to overcome severe depression, a permanent poor choice, or mental illness. We are saved by the life of Christ (see Hebrews 7:25). He doesn't leave us in our darkest hour, He's right there with us *pleading* to just give it more time... but many Christians think the pain will never end. They accept the lie of the enemy, one last time.

The passage from 1 John 5 in regard to the sin leading to death isn't suicide, it's unbelief. Unbelief in Christ's forgiveness is the only sin we cannot pray someone out of. They remain spiritually dead. Therefore we shouldn't beg God to *make* others believe. He won't do that. He never has. Instead we should pray for more opportunities which will influence them toward faith in Jesus.

So today, my friends, know this: Was Judas saved? I don't know. I sure hope he was. I'd like to meet him one day and talk about the things he saw as he walked with the Savior of the world. Not everything was recorded in Scripture so I know he'd have some good stories to tell.

A prayer for you: *Dear Jesus, I know it could've easily been me who betrayed you that night. I know you're a God of mercy and you loved Judas. You CHOSE him to follow you. So whatever you've decided, I trust you. You are never wrong. Right now, I lift up all who are reading this, directly to you. Acts 1:24-25 says you know the heart of every man, and when Judas was replaced he went to be where he belongs. This Scripture isn't clear about where that place is, but in my soul, I want to believe he went on to be with you. I know your grace abounds, not just for those who believed in you back then, but for today as well. There's no sin too big and no betrayal too strong which can possibly overpower your never-ending love for us. Amen.*

Day 22

The Truth About Those Who Have Fallen Away

"For it is impossible, in the case of those who have once been enlightened, who have tasted the heavenly gift, and have shared in the Holy Spirit, and have tasted the goodness of the word of God and the powers of the age to come, and then have fallen away, to restore them again to repentance, since they are crucifying once again the Son of God to their own harm and holding him up to contempt."

Hebrews 6:4-6

"Oh no. God, please no. I've fallen away! It's too late for me to repent!" Religious fear ruined my life for so long, I was even afraid to read my Bible. Certain verses would instantly petrify me like those goats who freeze when afraid—stiff as a board, falling over. Have you ever had a dream when you're so frightened you can't move? That's exactly how I felt because of false, fear-centered teaching.

I was taught to hold up certain individuals onto a pedestal because they were on stage behind a pulpit. It didn't matter what they said, I needed to believe it! They weren't teaching me the gospel; they may as well have been expounding on the life of Mickey Mouse. Truthful content wasn't the focus, the person teaching was, their *opinion* was, and don't you *dare* question them or you'll become the #1 enemy of the church! Rumors will fly about your disobedience and disrespect toward their *man* of God! Cold shoulders galore! Pastor-protecting vipers will strike vigorously, even if you *kindly* rebuttal their doctrine!

Unfortunately, I was influenced to believe blindly because their title was *pastor*, as if they had some special powers the rest of us didn't. I'm not bashing pastors, I love them very much. I'm bashing holding pastors *higher* than the rest of us. Some assemblies lift them up *so* high, Pastor So-and-So appears to be more important than Christ Himself. I'm not okay with this.

With all due respect to pastors—and although this gift is extremely important—the word *pastor* is only mentioned once in the New Testament. Don't you think if being pastor-focused was the gospel message, the epistles would be riddled with instructions toward this truth? Yet it's completely absent. Why?

Because we are all equal members of one Body.

Thankfully the Spirit of Christ didn't let me stay in such a fog of fake-grace, Covenant-mixing, and sometimes blatant lies about God. One of the most petrifying passages for me (taught out of context, of course) was found in Hebrews 6. The anti-Christ view of this section of Scripture goes like this:

If you sin too big or too often, as a Christian, it's too late for you. You can never repent your way back into grace. You have permanently fallen away from Jesus, now you're damned to hell.

Oh how Satan loved this. According to those who belittled the power of the Cross, this passage proved I sinned my way out of salvation all the time. *My* sinful actions and attitudes overrode the sufficiency of Jesus' sacrifice.

Who in the world do they think I am? As if a created being could possibly do *anything* greater than what Christ did. No wonder so many people hate Christians; it's because of garbage such as this. Enormous lies about the power of the blood of Jesus which cause horror and down-right hypocrisy.

Once the Holy Spirit began to teach me just how supreme Jesus' blood actually was and is, nobody could convince me that *any* sin in all the world, repeated or not, could Trump what the Cross has done.

"Lies, Matt! Hebrews 6 and Galatians 5 is clear! You can easily fall away from grace!"

Do you see how they shout? It's sad. Most who struggle with legalism have to be uber-aggressive, disrespectful, and condescending in order to get their point across. They puff up because deep in their own heart they *know* if what they're saying is true, then *they* are without hope as well. Yes, some are coy and passive-aggressive as they display their tendencies, but they too understand the bedrock of their theology is paper-thin. They know they fail every day. We all do. This is why James said, "We all stumble in many ways" (see James 3:2). But thanks be to God, we are not our failures, nor our successes.

There are only two spots in the New Testament with the words *fallen away*. They can be found in Hebrews 6 and Galatians 5. How about we look at both of them in context to discover we have nothing to fear? First, Hebrews.

Unlike any other epistle, the book of Hebrews created extreme confusion and terror for me until I understood the New Covenant. Now it's just plain beautiful! Here's what you need to know before you read a single word:

Christians have nothing to fear about anything written in Hebrews.

When we begin to feel panic as a believer while reading Scripture, we should pause and regroup in our mind. Don't forget what John taught us. If our feelings are fearful that's because we're imagining ourselves being punished. However, Jesus was already punished for us in full! God's love is perfect and casts out all fear! (See 1 John 4:18; from Paul: Romans 5:1,9, 6:23).

The truth about Hebrews is that it's meant to build confidence in the power of Jesus Christ, not cause believers to shake in our boots. There are zero threats for Christians in this writing, nor in any book of the Bible. The only threats are directed toward those who *reject* faith in Messiah. It's impossible for a Christian to do this because we've already been born again and our new supernatural birth is final. We can't reject being born because Jesus would have to die again—that's not happening (see Hebrews 1:3, 7:24-25, John 1:12-13, 3:6-7, 2 Timothy 2:13).

Without further ado, let's look at this "fallen away" section of the Bible. I'm going to underline what we really need to focus on for proper contextual exegesis:

> *"For it is <u>impossible</u>, in the case of those who have <u>once</u> been enlightened, who <u>have tasted</u> the heavenly gift, and <u>have shared</u> in the Holy Spirit, and <u>have tasted</u> the goodness of the word of God and the powers of the age to come, and then have fallen away, to <u>restore them again to repentance</u>, since they are crucifying once again the Son of God to their own harm and holding him up to contempt."* (Hebrews 6:4-6)

We must look at the whole of Hebrews to get the deepest context, not just these three verses—and we'll get to that. We must also zoom *in* on this single chapter, even though when this was written it wasn't broken down into chapters; this letter was one document, beginning to end. Chapters and verses were added hundreds of years later after the canon of the Bible was complete. This was done for easy searching and referencing, not to create what many context-twisters have demonically developed over time: *verse-itus.*

There are two different ways to look at Hebrews 6:4-6; in my opinion both can be true because both are centered on the authority of Jesus Christ. I have trusted New Covenant colleagues who see this section of Scripture completely different than one another, but both have the same result:

Christians are safe.

Before I list both views, let's be certain to understand that "falling away from grace" can only happen *in our identity* if we've never allowed grace to latch onto us. It is by grace we've been saved, through faith. Jesus *is* grace and *He* holds us secure (see John 1:17). It's never been about us holding onto Him, but the opposite. In fact, as much as it might hurt someone's ego, we're *not* holding onto Him by what we do or don't do. Such would negate grace completely (see Romans 11:6, Ephesians 2:8-9).

On the foundation of this truth, Hebrews 6:4-6 can have two views:

1. **This passage is describing an unbeliever who only *tasted* the truth but didn't *swallow*.** Unbelievers hear the gospel every day. Can this save them? No. They must believe Jesus has forgiven them of their sins, once, to be saved. Likewise with these home churches in the book of Hebrews; many Jews heard all about Jesus from the best gospel teachers, some who even walked with Him I'm sure. Disastrously,

many Hebrew unbelievers still wanted to go back to the Jewish temple to receive forgiveness by way of animal blood. They refused to repent in their belief system and instead hedged their bets on the works of the temple which were now obsolete *dead* works. If we read from the beginning of the chapter, the author expresses their exhaustion over re-explaining Old Covenant Mosaic theology which has been replaced with what Messiah has done. They *heard* the gospel, taste-tested it, were around people who were one with the Holy Spirit, but still wanted to stick with the traditions of Moses' commandments, therefore disgracing Jesus publicly. They tasted but wouldn't "drink in" the truth. The following passages emphasize their debacle.

2. **This passage is describing a Jewish Christian who *has* believed and the author is describing something which is *not* possible; they *can't* fall away from Christ back *toward* Mosaic legislative repentance.** This case can be built by reading from the opening of the chapter as *descriptive* not *pre*-scriptive. As in, this is describing someone who cannot *possibly* do the repentance required at the temple any longer *because* they've already repented toward faith in Jesus.

Either way we have the same result:

THE CHILD OF GOD IS FREE FROM ETERNAL DANGER BECAUSE OF JESUS.

If we keep reading, Hebrews 6:16-19 informs us that the promise between the Father and Son is final and *this* is the anchor for our soul! The legalistic Jew reading this letter needed to *stop* repenting from Mosaic customs and finalize their faith in Jesus. The ceremonial washing of hands, temple works, discussing the resurrection of the dead, and fear of eternal judgment? They needed to do a 180! They had to turn away from that stuff because it's worthless now that Christ has come!

Jesus is never going to offer His sacrifice again and again and again! The following chapters continue explaining these truths:

> Christ's blood is better than the blood of bulls and goats. Human Levitical priests not only die off but have to offer blood for their own sins, neither truth applies to Jesus. Christ is compared to Melchizedek, a person from their own scriptures who's without genealogy. The promise God made to their forefather, Abraham, and how that promise was fulfilled in Jesus, the author defines and clarifies. The importance of understanding and believing in the power and finality of the blood of Jesus *and* what it does *for* us and *to* us—such is spelled out plainly. Jesus Christ's *single* blood offering in the real temple in heaven forgives us *and* sanctifies us *and* makes us perfect—completely! This could never be done through the Mosaic Covenant! Read all the way through the book of Hebrews and these facts jump off the pages! It's all about Jesus and how the patriarchs and matriarchs longed for what we now have!

Jesus will never die again so we can be bold and confident! We don't need to shrink back toward the Law! Christ is the author and perfecter of our faith—not Moses! He's much greater than the old priesthood and repeated sacrifices! We have a once-for-all Sacrifice! We have a union with God through a single Mediator who lives forever!

As for the Galatians 5, "fallen away from grace" verse? We get the same result as we read it in the light of the Cross:

"You who are trying to be justified by the Law have been alienated from Christ; you have fallen away from grace." (*Galatians 5:4*)

There's no need to go deep into this passage, just read the entire chapter for context. Paul was furious over some Judaizers coming in behind his gospel teaching of Christ alone; they were attempting to mix in the Law *with* Jesus. He was so mad about their Covenant-mixture instructions he told them to cut off their genitals.

This is *not* Christians who blew it, but those who had been led astray in what they were being *taught*. Law. Moses. 613 commandments, not just ten plus tithing. This is the *same thing* the readers of Hebrews were being told to repent away from as well!

Christians cannot fall away from grace in their identity because their identity is one with the Son of God (see 1 Corinthians 6:17, Colossians 3:3). Can we fall away in our thinking? Yes. This is why we must preach Jesus Christ alone and Him crucified—not a drop of Moses. We love Moses, but his time was up at the Cross. Jesus replaced him (see 1 Corinthians 2:2, Galatians 3:2, 5:9, Hebrews 3:1-6, John 1:17).

So today, my friends, know this: Don't ever be afraid of falling away, believer. Jesus has such a tight grip on you there's nothing in all of creation that can open His hand (see John 10:28). Even when *you* think you've done this, you haven't. You too are created. You aren't more powerful than Him! (See Romans 8:38-39). Enjoy this blessed assurance and be yourself!

A prayer for you: *Father, today I'd like to give you thanks for the New Covenant. The promise you and Jesus made at the Cross, and you both*

being two unchangeable parties—God and God? I wish I knew this all along. I wish I understood that YOU are holding onto ME, not the other way around. You'll never let me fall away! What an amazing gift! Right now, I lift up all who are reading this, directly to you. For some, the New Covenant is starting to make sense! They've been taught a mixture, but your Spirit is sifting through the truth and lies in their minds! Take them deeper, Dad, so they can enjoy what Jesus did at the Cross even more! I also know there are unbelievers reading this. Keep letting them know how much you care for them. Keep knocking on their hearts, gently, as you always do. No matter if they're 9 or 90, you want to join them forever, and you will, by their one-time faith in Jesus! Amen.

Day 23

Jesus Is the Ultimate Scapegoat

"But the goat chosen by lot as the scapegoat shall be presented alive before the LORD to be used for making atonement by sending it into the wilderness as a scapegoat."

Leviticus 16:10

It's amazing to me how we Christians beg God for repeated forgiveness each day yet our Creator has never forgiven anyone through this method. I was taught, "God will forgive you, all you have to do is ask." The problem is, the words *ask for forgiveness* are not in the Bible—front to back.

God only forgives through blood, not words. We've adopted this theology of daily-forgiveness-begging by aimlessly trusting those who don't understand what the Cross has done. Just because someone is out of control, overly-emotional, or manipulatively sweet and gentle—therefore making us feel like crap—we don't *have* to believe them. Especially if their emotionalism is contrary to proper interpretation of Scripture in light of Jesus' finished work.

Even deeper, God only forgives by *faith* in blood, not by asking. We can ask, yes, but faith has to be the foundation of that original query. And if we *did* ask, He forgives us once and for all time, never again. If this weren't true then Old Covenant Judaism sounds much more appealing than Christianity. After all, the Hebrew people received forgiveness once a year at the Day of Atonement. I repeat, *once a year.*

On this side of the Cross the author of Hebrews explains how the Jews had their sin-slate cleaned prior to Messiah:

"In fact, the Law requires that nearly everything be cleansed with blood, and without the shedding of blood there is no forgiveness."
(Hebrews 9:22)

Israel, the Israelites, the Jews, the Hebrews (all the same group, the same race; we non-Jews are called Gentiles), they were forgiven of *every* sin for the previous year on the Day of Atonement. These men, women, and children had 613 rules to follow. When they broke one they didn't neurotically stop what they were doing and ask God to forgive them. Nor did they list off all their sins before bed, pleading with Yahweh for forgiveness as they promised to do better. Never did they confess to a priest, either. Not once is this recorded in the Old Testament. They had to wait.

The truth is, the priests were simply middlemen from one of their twelve tribes, the tribe of Levi. They were unemployed people who could only work at the temple. The tithe was meant to support them because they weren't allowed to have any other vocation. The Levitical priests would laugh if someone tried to merely confess sins to them. Blood *had* to be shed, and they all knew it.

The Jews also knew *when* they sinned those transgressions of the Law were "put on their books" so to speak. Each sin added up over the course of the year. As the following annual Day of Atonement arrived, they'd present their best animal to be slaughtered to pay off that sin-debt. The priest would then present that blood offering at the temple behind the curtain where only *they* were allowed to go.

What most Christians don't understand is that animal blood simply *atoned* for, or *covered up*, or *paid off* their past sins—never permanently taking them away. As soon as they walked down the stairs of the temple and broke one of the 613 commandments they'd need forgiveness again. For this exact reason such priestly duties had to be performed annually.

"Atonement is to be made once a year for all the sins of the Israelites."
(See Leviticus 16:34)

This passage from Leviticus is *before* Jesus came—keep that in mind. This was a commandment by Moses according to the Law, the Old Covenant. Sins had to be atoned for year after year because there was no way to remove them forever. The Jews were tired of this trip!

But wait! Christ did not *atone* for sins! He doesn't cover them up! He takes them away! Gone! He banishes them as far as the east is from the west! Even future sins are annihilated because He's not bound by time! He *created* time!

"It is impossible for the blood of bulls and goats to take away sins."
(Hebrews 10:4)

Do you see that? Animal blood cannot compare. John the Baptist, who never missed a Day of Atonement, when he simply *saw* Christ, the Spirit of God revealed the truth about Him:

The next day he saw Jesus coming toward him, and said, "Behold, the Lamb of God, who takes away the sin of the world!" (John 1:29)

HOW AMAZING! God, through Messiah, would choose to allow His blood to not just atone for sins but to throw them into oblivion!

"For I will be merciful to their iniquities,
And I will remember their sins no more." (Hebrews 8:12)

What if I told you, "I can see the future because I created the notion of time. I already know you won't always make the right choices, in fact, you'll make tons of mistakes. I can see them. But I'm still here for you. I'll never hold those faults against you. I've chosen to forgive you and I'll never leave you alone. Instead, I'll counsel you gently each day into the truth of who you truly are."

This is what God has done through His Son for all who will believe in Him *once*!

We've heard Jesus called the Lion, the Lamb, the Good Shepherd, and many other things. But did you know according to the Bible He's also a Goat? Don't confuse the "goats on the left sheep on the right" passage with a different section of Scripture about a goat found in Leviticus.

When a person believes Jesus has forgiven them they tap into *His* innocence. He did nothing wrong but was no longer innocent because He took on *our* sin. By way of Jesus being the greatest Scapegoat ever, we can blame all our mistakes on Him—we Christians *have* done this. This is why He lived! So the created people of the world can place their sins onto Him! He's our Scapegoat! A scapegoat is always innocent and removes all guilt!

The self-righteous individual sees this truth as a "license to sin" because they think they're doing a wonderful job at not sinning. HA! Christ said if we want to look to *not* sinning for righteousness we must be perfect like God! Good luck! (See Matthew 5:48). Juxtapose, the individual who knows they have sins only Jesus can remove once and for all time by His blood, we've seen this truth as life! We've seen *Him* as life! (See Colossians 3:3-4, John 10:28, 14:19).

We get the very word *scapegoat* from the Jewish Day of Atonement. If you get time, read all of Leviticus 16 and it's spelled out plainly. One ritual during this day required the priest to take two healthy goats and cast lots to decide which one would be used for the blood atonement, and the other, the scapegoat atonement.

The goat for the blood atonement was slaughtered; its blood then used behind the curtain in the temple to cover the people's sins for the previous year. The second goat was used to symbolically transfer the sins of the people *onto* the goat by the priest laying his hands on it. After he had "transferred" the sins onto the formerly-innocent-animal, he sent it off into the wilderness as the scapegoat which took their sins away—from the previous year—therefore symbolizing the take-away atonement. When the goat was far off into the distance and nobody could see it any longer the Jews erupted in celebration!

Unfortunately this had to be repeated annually—but only until Christ came! He one-upped the bloody goat *and* the scapegoat! He banished sins by *one* offering, Himself, thus causing the people to become perfect forever!

God was never *truly* pleased with animal blood. That blood simply reminded the Jews of how much they needed a Savior. They'd even burn the remains of the sacrificed animals, thinking such would bring God permanent pleasure. It did not. He only found *absolute* pleasure in His Son! (See Matthew 3:17). Those sacrifices and offerings were mere foreshadowings of what Christ would do with His own body and blood! He'd finish it all! Just look at this!

Therefore, when He (Christ) comes into the world, He says,
"Sacrifice and offering You have not desired,
But a body You have prepared for Me;
In whole burnt offerings and sacrifices for sin You have taken no pleasure.
"Then I said, 'Behold, I have come
(In the scroll of the book it is written of Me)
To do Your will, O God.'"

After saying above, "Sacrifices and offerings and whole burnt offerings and sacrifices for sin You have not desired, nor have You taken pleasure in them" (which are offered according to the Law), then He (Christ) said, "Behold, I have come to do Your will." He takes away the first (the Old Covenant) in order to establish the second (the New Covenant). By this will we have been sanctified through the offering of the body of Jesus Christ once for all.

Every priest stands daily ministering and offering time after time the same sacrifices, which can never take away sins; but He, having offered one sacrifice for sins for all time, sat down at the right hand of God, waiting from that time onward until His enemies be made a footstool for His feet. For by one offering He has perfected for all time those who are sanctified. (Hebrews 10:5-14, notes added)

So today, my friends, know this: Christian, *you* have been sanctified! *You* have been made perfect forever! How? By one offering! The body and blood of Jesus Christ! He's not *only* the innocent Scapegoat to blame, He's the Gate! He's the Vine! He's the Bread of Life! He's everything and He always will be!

A prayer for you: *Father, my goodness I get so excited when I write about this subject. Knowing that Jesus has removed all my sins brings such an explosion of enthusiasm from my fingertips! Thank you for revealing these truths to me! Right now, I lift up all who are reading this, directly to you. So many of these dear readers have just had a New Covenant lightbulb turn on in their minds. I remember when this first happened to me, finally realizing Christ's blood removed all my sins forever, causing me to become perfect? What a supernatural epiphany for us to enjoy! Take them deeper into this knowledge of Jesus! Remind them moment by moment what you've done to them because they've believed in your Son! In His mighty name I pray, amen.*

Day 24

When an Atheist Blames God

"But you must not forget this one thing, dear friends: A day is like a thousand years to the Lord, and a thousand years is like a day."

2 Peter 3:8

We have a lot of expectations for God.

"If you're real, then fix this!"

"If you love me you would *not* let this happen!"

"If you're so good then why am I in so much pain?!"

Such pleas can be heard from Christians, but if the atheist is honest, from them too. Most unbelievers don't believe because they have *such* high expectations for God—there's no way they'd trust Jesus.

"If God was real, this world wouldn't be in such bad shape! He'd *do* something!"

The fact of the matter is He *did* do something. He sent Jesus here. Further, He's *continuing* to do something through *us,* you and me, dear Christian.

Certain unbelievers think that if God was legitimate, heaven should be happening on earth right now—a utopia—with no questions asked. But because that's not the case, they refuse to believe in Messiah.

Aggressive antagonists' only defense is insulting God *because* this world is so painful—which is strange. Why insult something you don't think exists? Grandma used to say, "God has placed eternity in the heart of every man." She was quoting Scripture, even though I didn't understand this until I was older (see Ecclesiastes 3:11).

Like breathing, we can't *not* think, *Where'd I come from? Where will I go when I die?* It's impossible. This is what makes us different from the animal kingdom. We know we have a beginning and we know something will happen when our heart stops beating. Unbelievers will attempt to use the word *logic* but even their logic hits a dead-end road with this statement: "I came from something."

This, they can't deny. No human can. Something can't come from nothing. Every scientist will agree with those five words, even non-Christian scientists. So if we go all the way around the circle in a debate—*Where'd we come from?*—here's their unanswerable problem: *Atheists cannot explain our origin—the universe and humanity—without a god.*

They'll claim a loud bang happened, they've even named it—The Big Bang—*BANG!* And here we are. But they know that bang had to come *from* something. Why? Because they know something can't come from nothing. The most intelligent unbeliever will agree.

For this exact reason, Jesus said, "I am." (See John 8:58). No time frame. This is what makes God, *God*. He has no beginning or end. And what are we basing *time* on as we know it? His sun, His planets, earth's revolutions and rotations *around* the sun. He created these giant spheres and placed us at just the right distance so we don't burn up or freeze. The exact measurements are perfect to sustain human life. This isn't random but intelligently designed.

Our Creator made that big bang when He said, "Let there be light" (see Genesis 1:3). God made the first humans whom we've all descended from (see Genesis 1:27). The universe is not billions of years old. Non-believers came up with those numbers to discredit the timeline of the Bible. I don't know *how* old it is, but it's not billions or even millions. We don't need to worry about the age of Creation but instead focus on the love of our Creator.

Those who reject the God of the Bible do so because *if* He made this planet then why is it so messed up? The answer is He didn't make it messed up. He made it perfect. We, His creations, *humanity* messed it up (see Genesis 4:7, Romans 5:12). Thankfully, because He's not bound by time, He had a rescue mission planned before He spoke this into existence. The Bible says the Lamb was slain before the foundation of the earth! What?! *How*? How was Jesus sacrificed before the foundation of this planet?! (See Revelation 13:8).

Only by lifting ourselves up and out of time can this be understood. God can do that! (See 2 Peter 3:8). By not being bound by the very notion of time in which He created—based on the spinning of our planet around the sun—the Word, Jesus, planned on becoming one of His own creations! (See John 1:1-3, Colossians 1:15-19).

Why? To save us from the planet *we* jacked up with sin! (See John 3:16-18, Romans 5:12-15). Therefore our expectations *and* the Father's were placed on Him! Jesus came to help us! He came to save us! With His Spirit being in everyone who believes He's forgiven them, He works all things out for our ultimate good! (See 1 Corinthians 6:19, Romans 8:28). Even if we never get to see that good on this side of heaven, He is *for* you, He is *good*, and He's not *causing* your pain (see Hebrews 11, Romans 8:31).

So today, my friends, know this: Many unbelievers won't say it, but they want God to fix everything right now. They blame Him for what humanity has caused. They demand He never allow anything bad to occur—to them, or to the world they live in. But because that won't happen on this side of heaven, they feel the most disrespect they can give Him is to say He's not real. God, however, understands their frustration and still wants nothing but the best for them. His feelings aren't hurt, He's God. He can handle anything they throw at Him. He still loves them unconditionally (see Romans 5:8). He still wants them to come to the knowledge of the truth, believing in His Son as Savior (see 2 Peter 3:9, 1 John 4:19). Our Heavenly Father longs to have a close relationship with them, to comfort them. He wants all their expectations placed on Jesus, by grace through faith, once and for all time.

A prayer for you: *Father, today I'm grateful for this planet. I know that might sound strange, but what you've put together here is genius. What's more, in all your splendor, out of all your creations, we are your most prized possession and I know that. You built this for us! You created this planet and universe so we could live out our lives temporarily in these fragile bodies and then go on to live with you in your timeless realm. How cool is that?! Right now, I lift up all who are reading this, directly to you. For the unbeliever, keep letting them know how much you care for them. As they gaze up at the stars at night, remind them. As they look upon a beautiful mountain vista, remind them. As they hold their newborn baby, remind them. Remind them that these things were your ideas. Remind them that if they'll believe in Christ you'll be with them forever, starting now. Amen.*

Day 25

Should Women Be Silent, Submissive, and Cover Their Heads?

"There is no longer Jew or Gentile, slave or free, male and female. For you are all one in Christ Jesus."

Galatians 3:28

"You are a great leader."

"You were born to lead."

"You're different from other kids because you have tremendous leadership qualities. From the time you were a toddler I could tell, *you* lead."

These are just a handful of things I've said or written to my daughter, Grace, over the past 15 years. She's extremely unique in the fact that she's an alpha female—her temperament, that is. Grace is very loving and kind but she has a strong personality. Since she could walk and before she could talk, it was clear to me. She's no pushover. Her will is unmistakably powerful.

Grace is resilient. Grace is determined. Grace has a drive which will set her apart as she spreads her wings and soars about her life on earth. She means so much to me. My heart swells with adoration when I think about her gifts and who she is as a person—not just as my child.

For a moment, picture me calling her into the living room, sitting her down and saying, "Listen. I know you're intelligent, sweet, and steadfast, but if you ever decide that you want to *teach* about God, don't do it. You're not allowed because you're a female. The Bible forbids it. You need to be quiet because that's a man's job. Oh, and also, you need to be sure you cover your head. Scripture calls for it. Lastly, baby, when you get married, if your husband is an overbearing abusive monster who disrespects you, beats you up, is lazy, blows money, cheats on you and treats you like trash—you must *always* submit to him. Never talk back. And don't even *think* about having any type of career he disapproves of. Keep your attitude pleasant. Be soft, quiet, and flawlessly obedient to him. Okay? This is your role as a female. It's in the Bible."

Seems like I would need a huge boot planted directly in my rear, doesn't it? Yet this isn't far-fetched according to some who claim to be "men of God"—those who battle chauvinistic, disgusting tendencies, attempting to quote Scripture to prove the female gender isn't equal to them. How convenient!

Before I decided to address this topic I had to tell myself, "Now Matt, keep your cool when you write about those who don't see women equivalent to men." So the previous paragraph is about as animated as I'm going to get. I'm still maturing in how I react to certain behaviors coming from others. Therefore I must consciously *think* of these men with grace even when they disrespect *my* Grace because of her gender. But being graceful and loving *is* who I am. God remade me this way at salvation, just the same as He did all who've ever believed in Jesus (see Romans 5:5).

Today's date is May 11, 2020. In the news, not too long ago, a very famous male pastor was asked to describe a very famous *female* speaker and author. "Go home," was his response, with a chuckle.

Can you imagine that? This individual actually had the nerve to say she has no business doing what she's doing because she's a woman. He used Scripture to back up his bigotry—out of context, of course.

Isn't it handy to misinterpret words in the Bible to match up with egotistical dung? There are only three spots in the epistles which could possibly back up his claim. However, in order to come to such a discriminative determination we'd have to ignore everything Jesus stood for, every recorded interaction Christ had with women, as well as the heart of the gospel message.

Instead, we'd have to *focus on* demonic doctrine of inequality, subjugation, and covenant-mixture. Our teaching would have to include lies of sex-classes and keeping women in their rightful place of servitude as on-call baby-making objects. There's absolutely no other way to come to such a conclusion.

A person who struggles with pompous sexism might complain to me, "Read your Bible, Matt! Women are weaker than us! Women *can't* teach! Females are to be obedient, to serve, and to submit!"

Friend, I'll agree with *one* thing you said. Yes, let's read the Bible. First we'll view what was written to the Corinthians *in context* about women not being permitted to speak and submission. Pay special attention to what I've underlined as the bigot will overlook it:

> *For <u>God is not a God of confusion but of peace</u>. As in all the churches of the saints, the women should keep silent in the churches. For they are not permitted to speak, but should be in submission, as the law also says. <u>If there is anything they desire to learn, let them ask their husbands at home</u>. For it is shameful for a woman to speak in church.*

Or was it from you that the word of God came? Or are you the only ones it has reached? If anyone thinks that he is a prophet, or spiritual, he should acknowledge that the things I am writing to you are a command of the Lord. If anyone does not recognize this, he is not recognized. So, my brothers, earnestly desire to prophesy, and do not forbid speaking in tongues. But all things should be done decently and in order. (1 Corinthians 14:33-40)

The first thing I've underlined is *God is not a God of confusion but of peace.* This matters tremendously and gives Paul's frame of reference. The entire chapter, from beginning to end, he's correcting the church in Corinth for not having controlled, orderly gatherings. He informs them how to express spiritual gifts properly which should be in a well-behaved, thorough, understandable manner. He then addresses another concern: *women who were disrupting the group by asking their husbands questions in the middle of service.*

This is why Paul said wait and ask your husbands at home. Why? So there's not chaos. So people can learn and be edified in a peaceful environment. Imagine being in a church service or home gathering and everyone is talking, singing, speaking in tongues, and asking questions all at once. Outsiders would think we're crazy and reject the gospel because of *our* disorganized behavior (see 1 Corinthians 14:23).

Nothing was coordinated or managed. It was a no-holds-barred free-for-all. *This* was Paul's reasoning behind writing the aforementioned section of Scripture. Simply read from the beginning. It's undoubtedly evident.

Another passage used to berate women can be found in 1 Timothy 2. For context, look at what I've underlined closely:

I desire then that in every place the men should pray, lifting holy hands without anger or quarreling; likewise also that women should adorn themselves in respectable apparel, with modesty and self-control, not with braided hair and gold or pearls or costly attire, but with what is proper for women who profess godliness—with good works. Let a woman learn quietly with all submissiveness. I do not permit a woman to teach or to exercise authority over a man; rather, she is to remain quiet. For Adam was formed first, then Eve; and Adam was not deceived, but the woman was deceived and became a transgressor. Yet she will be saved through childbearing—if they continue in faith and love and holiness, with self-control. (1 Timothy 2:8-15)

At first glance, and if we don't pay close attention to the details, it would seem as if Paul is instructing Timothy to forget about the Cross completely. In essence, "Tim, just tell the women to sit down, shut up, don't wear flashy jewelry and to have babies to achieve their salvation."

Insane, yet some have built a doctrine on these *exact* ideas.

To begin with, we must understand why each epistle was written. That is, the situations surrounding the subject matter in each specific letter. We must consider *why* Paul wrote about certain controversies. He didn't waste ink on random topics but penned divine wisdom based on what *each* pocket of Christians were facing.

For this manuscript, Timothy was combating serious issues in his local assembly. His group was at war with an angry, quarreling, women's lib movement; females who wanted to overtake the congregation. Some historians claim they were worshipping the fake goddess, Diana.

This branch of the ecclesia, because of these feminists, weren't exuding any self-control, modesty, or wearing respectable apparel. In that culture, at that time, braided hair, gold and pearls, were viewed as licentious, rebellious accoutrement. Look at it this way, imagine if we had countless bikini-clad women entering our church gatherings today. It would be distracting. Such would be on par with those whom Paul was writing about.

These females were also saying Adam was deceived first in the Garden, not Eve, because Adam was an idiot. They argued that *he* was the original transgressing sinner.

"A woman would never do something so dumb!"

To make matters worse, they were claiming the ball-and-chain family life wasn't beneficial to their cause. For *this* reason Paul said childbirth saves them. As in, a peaceful, dignified life as a Christian wife is God's desire for them. Just start from the beginning of the chapter to see the big picture.

To digress even further, if we're going to look at this verse about childbirth saving a woman as literal, then forget about preaching Jesus. Just preach sex instead. Do you see the asininity in such a contorted thought? Birthing a child has never caused a person to be saved so that's obviously not the meaning.

The bottom line is, these women wanted to teach and exercise authority *over* the men. Not equal to, but dominant over. In this letter, Paul is fueling Timothy up with truth so he can gently debate such terrible heresy. He isn't establishing sexual discrimination. After all, the same author wrote *this* to the Galatian church:

> *"There is no longer Jew or Gentile, slave or free, male and female. For you are all one in Christ Jesus." (Galatians 3:28)*

We are one! This is the message of Jesus Christ which describes the Body *of* Christ! Just read Messiah's own words as He prays for the disciples and mentions us!

> *"My prayer is not for them alone. I pray also for those who will believe in me through their message, that all of them may be one, Father, just as*

> *you are in me and I am in you. May they also be in us so that the world may believe that you have sent me. I have given them the glory that you gave me, that they may be one as we are one—I in them and you in me—so that they may be brought to complete unity. Then the world will know that you sent me and have loved them even as you have loved me. (John 17:20-23)*

Wow! That's so beautiful! Jesus is praying for us! He's saying that *we* may be one! You and I, dear Christian! He said by becoming one He's giving *us* the glory! I repeat: HE GAVE *US* THE GLORY! This flies in the face of the legalist who barks, "Give God all the glory, not yourself!" But Christ said the opposite! He already *had* all the glory! He's God! He wants *us* to have *His* glory too! We do this by caring for one another as brothers and sisters! Not by saying anyone is greater or lesser! We enjoy and express the goodness of God by loving each other as the Father has loved Jesus!

I could explode with excitement!

Okay, I'll calm down ... *ahem*

... Now, before I put a ribbon on this devotional, I want to touch on one more passage many have used to harm women. In 1 Corinthians 11, there's a section about a woman covering her head. Supposedly, if she doesn't cover her head when she prays or prophesies it's dishonorable. First of all, this proves that women *can* speak because that's exactly what prophesy means in the New Testament letters—speaking, not future telling. Hebrews chapter 1 informs us that since Christ came future telling is now over. All the prophets of the Old Testament were future telling about the coming Savior. Now that He's here it's His Spirit who informs us of everything, not crystal-ball readers or prophets for profit. John even tells us this in the book of Revelation, to not *add* to anything (see Revelation 22:18-19).

But anyway, in 1 Corinthians 11, the head covering is not a doily, cloth, or burka. It's their actual *hair*. Verse 15 gives the complete context:

> *"but if a woman has long hair, it is her glory? For her hair is given to her for a covering?"* (1 Corinthians 11:15)

Again, we must keep the culture in mind from that time. Women with long hair were identified as being committed to a husband, whereas women with shaved heads were viewed as prostitutes. Just the same as provocative clothing is used for women-of-the-night *today*, back then the culture perceived shaved heads as, "I'm available for purchase."

We could put head coverings on a Satan-worshipping woman and pile them ten feet high, this would never cause her to be right with God. Such demonstrates the truth: *no head covering causes righteousness.* We're only righteous by grace through faith! By our new birth into the family of God! (See Ephesians 2:8-9, John 1:12-13, 3:6-8, 2 Corinthians 5:17,21).

So today, my friends, know this: God doesn't base our value on our gender but on His great love for us. I'd rather be taught by a woman who knows the love of God than by a man who doesn't. There are so many talented women who God wants to use in great ways! In fact, Jesus chose a woman to be the very first evangelist! (See John 4:4-30). The Kingdom of God is not patriarchal nor matriarchal but oneness in the love of Jesus Christ!

A prayer for you: *Heavenly Father, thank you for revealing the truth about just how important females are to you. In my heart, I already knew this, but you've taught me so much through your Spirit and Word. I now know*

that women aren't simply supposed to submit to men, but we're supposed to submit to them too. It's a mutual submission of love and respect. We're equal and I'm thankful for that. Today, I pray for my daughter, Grace. You know she's not a wallflower because you made her this way. As she lives her life and expresses who she is, protect her, guide her, and continue to empower her with your love. I know you will, Father. Remind her every day of just how gifted and important she is. Remind her how much she means to me too. Right now, I lift up all who are reading this, directly to you. So many of the early church leaders got it all wrong about women. Females were used as scapegoats and that's not okay. This twisting of Scripture and sexist teaching has been passed on from generation to generation in many churches. I ask that you begin to dilute this hellish ideology of women being inadequate. Infuse the truth into the minds of those who struggle with gender discrimination. I also ask for you to strengthen the battered women who've believed the lies of religious ogres for far too long. Empower them through your Spirit to STAND UP and be who you've recreated them to be in Christ! Through Him, they are courageous! Absolutely courageous! Amen!

Day 26

The Truth About Predestination (Part 1)

"I have been found by those who did not seek me; I have shown myself to those who did not ask for me."

See Romans 10:20

Biblical predestination is 100% true. However, the proper interpretation of what it actually *is* has confused the masses. Without beating around the bush, here are the differences:

- **False Predestination:** God has preselected only certain individuals to believe and be saved. Some of us are predestined for heaven and some for hell. We don't get to decide or participate in any way, shape, or form. Only God does.
- **True Predestination:** God has predestined the entire world to have the chance to believe and be saved not *just* the Jewish ethnic group. Gentiles—everyone on the planet who isn't Jewish—we too were predestined to be *invited* to join the family of God by grace through

faith in Jesus. Before the foundation of the universe, God's *predestined plan* was to summon both the Jew *and* the Gentile.

Simple enough, right? You'd think predestination would be uncomplicated, but oh my goodness, not at all. Many who obsess with Calvinism or Arminianism, as well as quite a few cults that wear a Christian hat, they'll vehemently argue about only certain *people* being chosen by God. Some even have a certain number of lucky individuals predestined to be saved. What a nightmare.

Calvinism says we have *no* choice; we're basically pre-programmed robots destined for heaven or hell. Arminianism says we *do* have a choice, but after choosing we're responsible for maintaining our salvation, as if the Father and Son's promise to one another at the Cross wasn't sufficient. Neither sounds like good news to me, yet the gospel literally means *good news*. I say we drop the "isms" connected to any man's name and focus on Jesus' Spirit to guide us into all truth.

So where have we gotten off base? As usual, poor interpretation of Scripture study while not being led by the Spirit. The Spirit will never lead us into error but only truth. Romans chapters 9-11 and Ephesians 1-3 are the foundational passages of predestination. Sadly, these scriptures have been contorted by demonic forces leading many to conclude God cherry-picks certain humans *to* believe and others *not* to believe.

Let's do some overview stuff to make predestination simple. Romans 9-11 is basically Paul calling out his racist Jewish kinsmen; he's telling them God decided to invite the Gentiles to be saved too. Here's a fictitious conversation that expresses what's happening:

"What do you mean, Paul?! You're telling us these disgusting Gentiles who know *nothing* about the Law, have *no* respect for Moses and the

Prophets, and have *never* sacrificed a *single* animal at the temple, you're saying God wants to include them too? Well that's not fair! We've worked way too hard to let this happen!"

"Yes. That's what I'm saying. God can have mercy on whomever He wants. Who are you to tell Yahweh what to do with humanity? You're simply one lump of clay in which He'll make many vessels from."

This conversation isn't in the Bible but I could easily picture it happening as Paul, a former devout Jewish man, revealed our Creator's intention of destroying Semitic segregation to Mosaic legalists. Their pious attitude was the reason they hung Jesus on the Cross and now Paul was saying they crucified the Messiah who *wants* to include non-Jews.

Romans 9-11 is Paul disclosing to his own flesh and blood that *they* are now without hope apart from Christ, not the Gentiles, but them. They've been broken off and need to be rejoined by faith. Their lineage means nothing now that Christ has come.

He begins by clarifying, in essence, saying, "God chose us in the past but now He's also chosen the Gentiles to be saved by way of the Christ who came from our bloodline."

Just look:

"For I could wish that I myself were accursed and cut off from Christ <u>for the sake of my brothers, my kinsmen</u> according to the flesh. <u>They are Israelites,</u> and to them belong the adoption, the glory, the covenants, the giving of the Law, the worship, and the promises. To them belong the patriarchs, <u>and from their race, according to the flesh, is the Christ,</u> who is God over all, blessed forever. Amen. But it is not as though the word of God has failed. For <u>not all</u> who are descended <u>from</u> Israel belong <u>to</u> Israel, and <u>not</u>

all are children of Abraham because they are his offspring" (See Romans 9:3-6)

Would Paul actually be cut off from Christ for the sake of his kinsman? No. This is a figure of speech expressing his deep desire for them to repent from the Law toward Jesus. He's telling them, "Just because you were born a Jew doesn't mean you belong to God any longer." They must believe Jesus to be included *with* the Gentiles who *have* chosen Him by faith.

"This means that it is not the children of the flesh who are the children of God, but the children of the promise are counted as offspring." (Romans 9:8)

The children of the flesh are the Jews, Israel. Not the modern geographic location of Israel because it wasn't established until 1948—but their *race*. Further, Paul isn't referring to *the* flesh, or *sarx*, as he did in Romans 7 and 8, but actual physical DNA; *human* lineage.

Juxtapose, the children of the promise is you and I, dear Gentile. God made a promise to Abraham before the Law, before Israel was even formed through Moses after the Hebrew Exodus from slavery in Egypt. Even deeper, God made a promise to Abraham *before* he had a *single* child. As an old man, God guaranteed him this:

"I will make you the father of many nations." (See Genesis 17:4)

MANY NATIONS! Not just the Jewish nation but *many* nations! Where would those nations come from? The entire world! Asians, Indians, American Indians, Europeans, Incas, Africans, Canadians, Eskimos,

Antarcticans—absolutely every nation on the planet who didn't follow Moses through the Red Sea floor! God predestined us to have the chance to be saved!

We are the fulfillment of God's promise to Abraham! We are the children of the promise! Since Jesus came it's no longer just about Israel but *we too* were predestined to join God by way of His Son through belief!

Unfortunately the Jews hated Paul because he told them *they* would serve *us*, not the other way around. Why? Because Christ came through the tribe of Judah. Judah was one of the twelve tribes of Israel.

"The older will serve the younger." As it is written, "Jacob I loved, but Esau I hated." (See Romans 9:12-13)

The *older* is the Jews. The *younger* is the Gentiles. His symbolism is clear.

Another epiphany Paul would reveal is that after we place our faith in Jesus we're no longer Jew *or* Gentile but a whole new creation in Christ! (See Galatians 3:28-29, 2 Corinthians 5:17).

In Romans 9:13, from above, Jacob signified the Jews, Esau signified the Gentiles. During the time of Jacob and Esau, which was before Christ came, it was God's prerogative to choose the Jews and *not* choose the Gentiles to carry His oracles and Messianic bloodline. It was God's prerogative to temporarily harden Pharaoh's heart in order to preserve the pedigree of Judah in which the Word would become flesh.

"Who are we to tell God what to do?" was the message of Paul, yet the Jews still rejected his communication about Christ.

Even in the book of Acts, as he preached to his countrymen, they shunned his news of Jesus therefore rejecting eternal life. He preached *first* to them, and *second*, preached to the Gentiles, but only *after* the Jews refused to believe (see Acts 13:45-48). This proves that predestination is not God forcing people to believe and leaving others without hope, including Israel. They still have time to repent and believe.

"No way, Matt! Jesus even said many are called but few are chosen!"

Yes, friend, Jesus did say that. But in context He's referring to the copious amount of Jews *first* being called and *still* refusing to join Him. The Jews are *the many*, the Gentiles are *the few*. Those who were originally called by God through Moses rejected Him; *we* who are the few, were then *chosen* because we believed. Read the entire parable, not just a single verse, to find out the truth (see Matthew 22:1-14).

"Matt, you're so wrong! You gotta be caught up in the elect and only smart people know that! You're wasting your time!"

Do you see how the enemy can make us angry and anxious when we *think* we must be part of a preselected group? Yet Christ said His yoke is easy and His burden is light (see Matthew 11:28-30). The truth is, the elect is the corporate body of Christ, not a fated group of humans. In fact, we believers are *all* part of a royal priesthood of saints! We're equal because we were chosen to have the chance to believe—and we did!

> *"But you are a chosen people, a royal priesthood, a holy nation, God's special possession, that you may declare the praises of him who called you out of darkness into his wonderful light." (1 Peter 2:9)*

We were chosen because Israel rejected God and He wanted to add to His family! We believed in Christ for the forgiveness of our sins and instantly became a royal group of His special possession! This happened by grace through faith, not by random chance!

Day 27

The Truth About Predestination (Part 2)

"This mystery is that the Gentiles are fellow heirs, members of the same body, and partakers of the promise in Christ Jesus through the gospel"

Ephesians 3:6

The person who struggles with electionism will say Scripture proves that God decides who He'll love and who He'll hate based on *Jacob I loved, Esau I hated,* but that's not Paul's point. His argument is for the defense of his ministry which included the Gentiles.

This extremely arrogant group of non-believing Jews, his own family and friends, he wanted them to understand God will have mercy on whomever He wants. They're no better than anyone else.

The clay doesn't get to tell the Potter what to do with the clay. If the Potter wants to use different lumps of clay however He sees fit, it would serve the clay well to remember who controls the shaping of everything (see Romans 9:18-25).

We are creat*ed*. He is Creat*or:*

"And he is not served by human hands, as if he needed anything. Rather, he himself gives everyone life and breath and everything else." *(Acts 17:25)*

The bottom line is, God wanted to include the Gentiles and the Jews were salty about it. They thought they could boss Him around and tell Him who to pick. Nope.

Although, the Jews *were* correct about a couple things:

1. God never included Gentiles in the past, as far as the Old Covenant was concerned.
2. The Gentiles weren't working according to the Law, striving for righteousness by obeying 613 commandments—not just ten.

Yet God now has the "audacity" to bring in the Gentiles by grace through faith? Oh yeah! That's exactly right! *This* is predestination!

Those who were not my people I will call "my people" (See Romans 9:25)

"What shall we say, then? That Gentiles who did not pursue righteousness have attained it, that is, a righteousness that is by faith; but that Israel who pursued a law that would lead to righteousness did not succeed in reaching that law. Why? Because they did not pursue it by faith, but as if it were based on works." (See Romans 9:30-32)

Many of the Jews were working, not believing. Many of the Gentiles were now believing, not working. To the Jews this was extremely heretical. Such is the same for many of today's devout church-goers who snarl at the stench of "sinners" while fluffing themselves up through rah-rah dog-and-pony shows.

The stumbling block of Jesus Christ was now tripping up zealous, legalistic Hebrew people who thought their "amazing" behavior caused them to be right with God. Grievously, for them, faith was now the end of the Law for all who would believe in this stumbling block! (See Hebrews 9:32-33, 10:1-4). I could just hear them quoting the Psalms as they fought back, "Paul, you need to be killed for such blasphemy! We are to meditate on the Law day and night! We are to *love* the Law as David did!"

He'd rebut with a truth from Hebrews 6:1, "I'm sorry, but you must repent from your dead works toward Jesus."

In Romans 10 and 11 he goes on to explain how important it is that his kinsmen shift from their disobedience of refusing to believe. Why? Because *they* were now cut off from God and the believing Gentiles had been grafted in. Of course, they too could be grafted *back* in but they must turn from the Law toward faith in the Son of God. Trampling on the Spirit of Grace and looking to temple sacrifices for forgiveness would not end well for them (see Hebrews 10:26-29).

How many Bible-thumping, unloving people would be furious if you told them, "A prostitute who believes Jesus has forgiven them is just as holy as Jesus."? (See 1 John 4:17). Now multiply that by 100 and you'd get a taste of what Paul was facing.

He opens up his letter to the Romans informing them that no unbelieving Jew *or* Gentile has any excuse *not* to believe. The Jews had the Law, which showed them their need for a Savior, we Gentiles had our consciences. Both parties are without hope apart from Christ (see Romans 2:12-15).

Let's jump to Romans 8:29-30 to see the cusp of predestination:

> *"For those whom he foreknew he also predestined to be conformed to the image of his Son, in order that he might be the firstborn among many brothers. And those whom he predestined he also called, and those whom he called he also justified, and those whom he justified he also glorified."*

This passage confirms God predestined everyone who will believe in Jesus to grow and mature in Him! We have a calling which is to bear the fruit of the Spirit! (See Galatians 5:22-23). Eventually we'll be completely glorified in our physical body (see 1 Corinthians 15:35-58), but for now, we've been glorified in our soul and spirit. We've been preselected to do this as believers on earth. God can see the end from the beginning and He's already worked this plan out. He's not *controlling* this plan but working it *through* us *with* us in a relationship. Collectively, as a church body, God is conforming our actions and attitudes *into* the image of His Son!

With this foundation set about predestination from Romans, Ephesians 1-3 can easily be deciphered through the Spirit. Once again, Paul is explaining the same mystery to those in Ephesus as he did to the Romans:

God has released the gospel onto the entire world, not just the Jews.

As we look at these verses, keep in mind, when he uses the word *we* he's referring to the Jews. When he uses the word *you* it's directed at the Gentile Ephesians. When he writes *us* he's pointing at the new creation, neither Jew nor Gentile but those who've believed in Christ for salvation.

> *"he chose <u>us in him</u> before the foundation of the world, that we should be holy and blameless before him. In love <u>he predestined us</u> for adoption to himself as sons through Jesus Christ, according to the purpose of his will, to the praise of his glorious grace (See Ephesians 1:4-5)*

All of humanity was predestined to have the opportunity to believe Jesus after He was crucified, buried, and resurrected. Predestination is about being *in* Him, *in* Jesus, *in* His actual Spirit. This is the mystery which wasn't revealed until the gospel was released onto the Gentiles through Paul. He was the first Jew to reach out to non-Jews with the good news; a mystery which was the will of God all along!

This apostle to the Gentiles unraveled the enigma! Both the Jew *and* the Gentile could now join him *in* Christ!

> *"In him we have redemption through his blood, the forgiveness of our trespasses, according to the riches of his grace, which he lavished upon us, in all wisdom and insight making known to us the mystery of his will, according to his purpose, which he set forth in Christ as a plan for the fullness of time, to unite all things in him, things in heaven and things on earth. In him we have obtained an inheritance, having been predestined according to the purpose of him who works all things according to the counsel of his will, so that we who were the first to hope in Christ might be to the praise of his glory. In him you also, when you heard the word of truth, the gospel of your salvation, and believed in him, were sealed with the promised Holy Spirit, who is the guarantee of our inheritance until we acquire possession of it, to the praise of his glory." (Ephesians 1:7-14)*

> *"And you were dead in the trespasses and sins… " (See Ephesians 2:1)*

> *"But God, being rich in mercy, because of the great love with which he loved us, even when we were dead in our trespasses, made us alive together with Christ—by grace you have been saved" (Ephesians 2:4-5)*

I've underlined *being rich in mercy* because those who see the first few chapters of this epistle as God hand-selecting people to be saved, let me ask, *how* could He be rich in mercy? He couldn't. There's no mercy in such a twisted view of predestination.

It's *because* God is rich in mercy He included those who were close to Him, the Jews, because they had the first Covenant. But He also chose those who were far off and had *no* Covenant with Him, the Gentiles. This would include me because I'm not Jewish:

"remember that at that time you were separate from Christ, excluded from citizenship in Israel and foreigners to the covenants of the promise, without hope and without God in the world. But now in Christ Jesus you who once were far away have been brought near by the blood of Christ." (Ephesians 2:12-13)

We Gentiles weren't there at the base of Mount Sinai, promising God we'll do everything written in the Book of the Law (see Exodus 19:8, 24:7). The Jews were, yet they failed at holding up such a promise to God. The hostility of the righteous requirements of the Law—perfection or bust—were now torn down! (See Matthew 5:48, James 2:10, Galatians 3:10, Colossians 2:13-17). The same 613 commandments which alienated Jews from Gentiles, that *curse* was banished through Christ! He brought us together as one!

"For he himself is our peace, who has made us both one and has broken down in his flesh the dividing wall of hostility by abolishing the law of commandments expressed in ordinances, that he might create in himself one new man in place of the two, so making peace, and might reconcile us both to God in one body through the cross, thereby killing the hostility. And he came and preached peace to you who were far off (Gentiles) and peace to those who were near (Jews). For through him we both have access in one Spirit to the Father. So then you are no longer strangers and aliens, but you are fellow citizens with the saints and members of the household of God" (See Ephesians 2:14-19, my notes added in parenthesis)

So today, my friends, know this: Jesus said, "When I am lifted up from the earth, I will draw all people to myself" (see John 12:32). This *has* happened *at* the Cross! Nobody can come to Him unless God draws them, so He drew you! (See John 6:44). Before Christ, this was still a mystery! But now the final Piece who brought peace has caused the predestination puzzle to be solved!

"This mystery is that the Gentiles are fellow heirs, members of the same body, and partakers of the promise in Christ Jesus through the gospel" (Ephesians 3:6).

A prayer for you: *Heavenly Father, thank you for your predestined plan to give me redemption through the opportunity to believe in Jesus. What a merciful and graceful plan! Right now, I lift up all who are reading this, directly to you. So many of these dear people have enjoyed what they've just read, yet for others this is hard to believe. I ask that you open up their minds to the truth of your gospel. Let them know if you pre-picked certain people to be saved, then all the passages in the Bible about evangelism, warnings of hell, and believing, would be worthless. After all, you'd have everything rigged so we should just eat, drink, be merry, and hope you picked us. And Dad, for those who arrogantly "feel picked," remind them they too must believe in Christ no matter how they feel. But for those who don't feel picked, let them know they have the chance to believe right now. Today is their day of salvation! In Jesus' name I pray, amen.*

Day 28

Why Did Jesus Get Angry and Flip Tables?

"In the temple courts he found people selling cattle, sheep and doves, and others sitting at tables exchanging money. So he made a whip out of cords, and drove all from the temple courts, both sheep and cattle; he scattered the coins of the money changers and overturned their tables."

John 2:14-15

Bear with me while I quote some garbage:

"Jesus flipped the tables to show you He's not putting up with *your* crap! Don't repent? That's what you'll get!"

"Jesus had *righteous* anger over *you* trying to make money! That's why He turned the tables!"

"You can't sell merchandise and coffee in your church! How *dare* you! Christ would come in here and flip all this over!"

"Jesus turned the tables to *prove* He was no pushover! So I'm going to do the same and *whoop, your, butt*!"

My stomach turns a little, just typing that dung. But I've heard it all in regard to Jesus getting angry, making a whip, flipping tables, and driving people out of the temple courts.

For the immature individual who doesn't understand the New Covenant, pushes Law, and expresses no self-control, table-flipping Jesus is their go-to passage when they want an excuse to act like a jerk. They'll pull this section of the Bible up and out of context, "What would Jesus do?! He'd knock you on the head, that's what!"

No friend, He wouldn't. On this side of the Cross He's wooing unbelievers not trying to cause them pain, and He never *did* try to cause them pain. Jesus doesn't bring tragedy onto a person and then swoop around to the backside of that tragedy to comfort them. What a monster He would be. This world brings enough trouble on its own. He came to save us from it, not heap on more heartache.

So what *is* the proper context behind the actions of Jesus Christ that day? Did He go berserk because they were gambling, price gouging, or conducting business on holy ground?

Here's the truth: *He was standing up for you and me, dear Gentile.*

This *one* section of the temple was designated for non-Jews. We weren't allowed to go anywhere else except this small area *to pray*. The Gentiles who came to this part of the temple courts believed in Yahweh—the God of the Jews—but knew they weren't included in their Covenant.

They didn't follow Moses out of Egypt, they didn't walk through the muck of the bottom of the sea, nor did they promise God they'd do everything written in the Book of the Law (see Exodus 19:8, 24:3). Yet they still *believed* in God. They had faith. Faith is what has always justified a person, not the Law, but that subject is for another day (see Romans 1:17, Galatians 3:11, Hebrews 10:38).

Jesus knew this one small part of the temple gave them hope. Jesus knew that many Gentiles who were saved by faith went there to pray. It was a place of prayer *for them*; a geographic location of comfort, of longing for something better than being rejected because of their race. The promise God made to Abraham before Israel was even formed, this area of the temple was specifically designed for *that* promise (see Genesis 22:15-18).

Jesus saw what the Jews had done by desecrating this zone of the promise for the Gentiles to be saved! They cared *nothing* about the Abrahamic promise and He was hot! The promise God made to Abraham, that he would be the father of *many* nations through Abraham's seed (Jesus)—not *just* the nation of Israel—was being snuffed out by money-hungry bigots! (See Galatians 3:29).

Just look at what Jesus said to these fools who were cashing in on the Law of Moses by setting up shop in the Gentiles' section of the temple:

> *And as he taught them, he said, "Is it not written: 'My house will be called a house of prayer for all nations'? But you have made it 'a den of robbers.'" (Mark 11:17)*

Christ was quoting two of their *own* prophets from their *own* scriptures—Jeremiah and Isaiah! I could picture Him yelling at them:

> "ALL NATIONS! AAAAAAAAAAAALL NATIOOOOOOOONS! NOT JUST YOURS!"

He was mad. Very mad. His own people, their own sacred writings which foretold about God including the Gentiles too, they were stomping on that. They would rather make money off the need for animals than realize Jesus would remove that need forever in Himself which would bring in *everyone* (see Hebrews 10:4,10-14, John 1:29, 19:30, Galatians 3:28).

So today, my friends, know this: Jesus got angry and flipped tables because He was passionate about including all nations in with His family, not just the Jews who believed. Not one time in the Bible does Jesus get mad at a Gentile who reached out to Him. He only got mad at the legalists who refused to include us. They wanted religion but Jesus wanted relationship. Christ got livid when this promise was ignored. He's still passionate about this *very* promise, today. Through you and I, dear Christian, He's still reaching out to everyone who has not yet believed. Keep being yourself. You are fulfilling the original promise of God, to include the entire world in His family, by grace through faith.

A prayer for you: *Dad, thank you for giving me the right to call you Dad. I had an enraged person email me the other day, irate about the fact that I call you Dad. But that's what you are. You're my Dad. You're my Father. You're Abba. I love you so much and I'm so happy you gave me the right to be your son, even as a Gentile. Right now, I lift up all who are reading this, directly to you. So many of these dear readers have the wrong idea about you. Because of people who've misrepresented you they've believed the lie that you're furious, yet you're not. All your fury was placed on Christ at the Cross. Instead, you're enthusiastic about including all nations, all people groups, and every ethnicity in heaven. Keep using our hands, feet, and mouths to accomplish this amazing feat. We're honored, Dad. Amen.*

Day 29

Will Bible Teachers Be Judged More Harshly?

"For we are co-workers in God's service; you are God's field"

See 1 Corinthians 3:9

People. An audience. Those we've pointed to Christ and have been saved through what we've taught. This is the true contextual reward found in 1 Corinthians 3. I'll go deeper into this passage shortly, but first, I've heard it said Bible teachers will be judged by God in two different ways:

1. *with greater strictness*
2. *twice on Judgement Day (once for what Jesus did, second for what they taught)*

This can't be true unless we're overlooking the good news of the gospel, for such turns teaching into a work. If *anything* is a work it's not based on grace because Paul called the gospel the gospel *of* grace (see Romans 11:6, Ephesians 2:8-9, Acts 20:24).

Just imagine God saying, "I'm so disappointed in you, for what you taught. But you're still saved, so squeak in through the back door." Or, "You did such a great job with your Bible teaching! Here's an extra reward!"

Some even claim, "Teachers are held to a higher standard!" but that's not biblical due to the fact that Christ *is* our standard. Sure, we may be held to a higher standard by religious nut-jobs, but not by God. His yoke is easy and His burden is light. His commandments are not burdensome (see Matt 11:30, 1 John 5:3).

Friend, we can rest assured, when we physically die God won't have a look of disappointment on His face, nor do we have to worry about missing out on any reward. Why? THE CROSS.

With all due respect and love, saying we'll be judged for our teaching is double-talk and ignores the sufficiency of Christ's work. Saying we'll be judged in a negative way—for anything, let alone our teaching—causes fear for the person who's brave enough to actually teach. Double-talk doesn't come from God. Fear doesn't come from God. Hence, this special "teacher judgment" is error.

Let's look at the passages used to create this theology:

1. **James 3:1 *"Not many of you should become teachers, my brothers, for you know that we who teach will be judged with greater strictness."*** At first glance it would seem James is saying God will judge Bible teachers brutally, but that's not the context. First of all, the Bible wasn't yet compiled when this was written, therefore Bible teaching *can't* be the context. So we must back up to find out who this is written to and why, *then* we can understand chapter 3 quite easily. James directed this epistle toward the Jews who were still skeptical

about faith in Christ—*not* believers. He's doing the same thing Jesus did in the Sermon on the Mount: *exposing the true standard of the Law so they would repent toward grace.* This is addressed "to the twelve tribes" (see James 1:1). Who were the twelve tribes? Israel. The Jews. What did the twelve tribes perpetually teach? The Law. James is saying if you want to be judged with greater strictness from both God and people keep teaching the Law. We Christians don't do this, we teach Jesus. Jesus and the Law oppose one another as polar opposites (see John 1:17). This passage isn't pointed at us so we have nothing to fear. New Covenant grace teachers make mistakes all the time, and that's okay (see James 2:10, 3:2, Galatians 3:10, Romans 5:20).

2. **1 Corinthians 3. *The whole chapter.*** I'm not going to quote the entire chapter so please read it if you get time. Now, it would *seem* as if Paul is saying teachers will be judged by fire on Judgment Day—still saved though—and they'll get rewarded or the opposite for what they taught; a "teacher evaluation" so to speak. But I'm not seeing that. Again, this would negate everything Jesus stood for and create a new "teacher works amendment" to the gospel. Will God condemn us or show favoritism for what we teach? No. There's no condemnation for His children and our only reward is the reward of the inheritance—Christ in us! We're enjoying Him right now! (See Romans 8:1, Colossians 1:27, 3:4). Can God be let down by Bible teachers or hand them extra credit based on 1 Corinthians 3? Remember, the Bible wasn't canonized until many years after this was written, so "special Bible teacher judgment" isn't credible. We all teach some sort of error, worrying about being judged for that error is wrong. Jesus was already judged for *all* our errors, not just for teaching but for everything. Further, what is a disappointment to God? A sin. What has Jesus done with those? He's taken them all away for everyone who

has believed (see John 1:29, 19:30). What I see from 1 Corinthians 3 is Paul rebuking a group of immature Christians for having "favorite teacher factions." Some liked one teacher and others didn't, and vice versa. Paul's informing them the teacher isn't as important as the teacher's *message*. Whatever isn't true *in their message* will burn up—not them, but their message. So what's the reward he's referring to if it's not the reward of the inheritance? Simple: *an audience of believers on earth and in heaven as a result of teaching the truth!* The people are the field and the teachers are the co-workers in that field! (See 1 Corinthians 3:9). We aren't teaching for extra rewards but for human beings to come to know Jesus! WE WANT PRISONERS TO BE SET FREE! When we've helped someone understand how much Jesus loves them by way of something we've said or written, it's extremely rewarding! Paul's exhorting them to stop fighting over who's the best teacher, in essence, "Grow up! Would you?" Read all the way to the bottom of the chapter and he finishes the topic like this, "So then, no more boasting about human leaders!" (See 1 Corinthians 3:21).

3. **Galatians 5:10. *"I am confident in the Lord that you will take no other view. The one who is troubling you will bear the judgment, whoever he may be."*** What's the entire frame-of-reference behind the letter to the Galatians? Law teachers infiltrating a church in which Paul had already established the truth of Jesus Christ alone. The "other view" is the Law. The contrast of the entire book is Mosaic legalism versus the Spirit of Christ. Paul was *furious* about this! He even called the readers fools and told the Law teachers to castrate themselves (see Galatians 3:1, 5:12). That's how serious he was about not mixing Law in with the gospel. Those who planted seeds of Moses in his garden of grace are the people who "will bear the judgment"—not Christians. What did James say about Law teachers? They'd be judged strictly,

> according to what they teach. Do Christians teach the Law? No, only unbelievers do. If a Christian does teach the Law *with* Jesus, His Spirit keeps them saved and continually counsels that person away from such mixture. But it's still their choice to quit legalism completely. A concoction of Law and grace within the mind of a child of God will never feel right. They won't enjoy peace until they repent of not only trusting Christ for His forgiveness but also for His morality. Accordingly, Galatians 5:10 isn't directed at you and I, believer, but Judaizers; those who were hung up on Moses and didn't have faith in Jesus.

If you think about it, if Bible teachers were judged for their teaching, how can we determine if someone is officially a Bible teacher? The legalist will tell you, but what's the truth? Is it when we teach once, twice, or 1,000 times? Is it when we graduate from cemetery—I mean, seminary? Did Paul, Peter, James, Jude, and John go to seminary? What about Matthew, Mark, and Luke? No? So were *they* teachers? Should we turn from teaching if we think we're in error, never teach again, go home and repent? How can we be 100% sure we've repented properly *from* teaching? Is it based on casual conversation or do we have to be on stage and then off stage? Does social media count?

Do you see it? Do you see how this notion of Bible teachers being scolded or handed extra goodies for what they said or wrote isn't the truth? Thankfully, I sure do. If I didn't you'd never hear from me again. Instead, I'd go work on my golf swing and spend more time with Jennifer and Grace. I'd never take the chance of getting a frown from God on Judgment Day. But that's *not* the truth. Therefore I'll continue until the wheels fall off because I enjoy this very much.

So today, my friends, know this: Teach all you want and don't be afraid. Learn, grow, mature, take chances, fall down, get up, and move forward fearlessly! Use what you've got! It is enough! Use what you know! IT IS

ENOUGH! God is always, always, *always* proud of you! Don't worry, everything that's not the truth will burn up like wood, hay, and stubble. The fire and refinement of the Cross will do all the work in regard to your message. You can rest knowing that Christ is sifting through your message with unlimited patience, counsel, and care. You can be yourself. On the day you meet Him face to face He won't pull you aside to correct your teaching errors, oh no. He'll never reference any of your sins. He'll greet you with the warmest smile you've *ever* seen. He'll look you in the eyes, hug you, and say, "Welcome home. I'm so glad you're here."

A prayer for you: *Father, thank you for the truth of the gospel. It has taken so much pressure off me. Knowing that no matter what I do or don't do, I'm secure because of Jesus? This is empowering! Right now, I lift up all who are reading this, directly to you. Dad, you know who has just read this devotional, and you know who needed to. I pray that you take them further into the awareness of what Jesus has done. Help them enjoy the freedom He died to give them, and if they want to teach, encourage them to teach. Amen.*

Day 30

How to Fulfill the Great Commission

"I am sending you to open their eyes, so that they may turn from darkness to light and from the power of Satan to God, that they may receive forgiveness of sins and a place among those who are sanctified by faith in me." ~Jesus

See Acts 26:17-18

Over the centuries, countless Christians have been pressured into "attempting" to fulfill the Great Commission. Pressure to save the world can be absolutely terrifying, yet terror doesn't come from God. Love does. Growth does. *Maturity* does. Does a vine pressure a branch to produce fruit? Of course not, and this is the example Christ used to describe our relationship with Himself, as does Paul (see John 15:5, Galatians 5:22-23).

The problem so many believers have is that it's hard to shake pressure-filled thoughts because of life-long pressure-filled teaching, especially about evangelism. Grievously, the Great Commission has been contorted to match up with anti-Cross theology by way of two main conundrums:

1. Mixing the Covenants.
2. Not viewing everything in the Bible, front to back, through the lens of the finished work of Jesus.

The assignment of the Great Commission given by Christ in Matthew 28 is beautiful! But the *delivery* when not given properly insights anxiety. Anxiety morphs into hypocrisy, hypocrisy into anger, anger then repels the lost and frustrates the saints.

We are the saints, you and I, dear Christian, *evenly*. Saint means holy one, holy means sanctified, sanctified means set apart, and that is what we are! We've been set apart from the world, sin, and death by being placed inside of God's very own Spirit! (See Hebrews 2:11, 10:10,14, Acts 26:17-18, Romans 1:1, 8:2,9, Colossians 1:22, 3:3-4).

We are not sinners saved by grace! A sinner is what we *were* but we've been crucified with Christ! (See Galatians 2:20). Believers are never described as sinners in Scripture, we're always addressed as saints! (See Romans 1:7, 1 Corinthians 1:2, 2 Corinthians 1:1, Ephesians 1:1, Philippians 1:1, Colossians 1:2, 1 Thessalonians 3:13, 2 Thessalonians 1:10, and more).

We are saints who forget we are saints, therefore we sin. But *sinner* is not our identity in any way, shape, or form because God gave us a sinless identity at salvation. This was the only way He could permanently make His home in us. If we were still sinners He'd still be "coming and going" like He did in the Old Testament, but Christ has made us brand new! (See Psalm 51:11, Romans 6:6-10, 2 Corinthians 5:17,21).

Sure, Paul called himself the chief of sinners but he was describing his past life as an unbeliever who persecuted Christians. Read around that passage for the full context (1 Timothy 1:12-17). After all, Paul's the one who wrote the most about us *being* saints! The sooner we start telling the truth about what God has done to us, the sooner sinning will no longer be our focus. Expressing love, morality, and righteousness will be because such is fitting for saints.

Thankfully, the Great Commission isn't an individual assignment to be strived for or achieved. Instead, it's the corporate goal of the saints; the organic ambition of the body of believers as a whole. The Great Commission *will* be accomplished inevitably as we reveal our true nature as members of God's household. By allowing Him to live through us—through our hands, feet, mouths, and minds—we *are* fulfilling what Christ commanded *in* the Great Commission.

Many well-meaning saints get tripped up on the word *command* or *commandment*, confusing Jesus' directives with Moses'. Moses' commandments tallied 613, according to the Old Covenant. Jesus', according to the New Covenant, only has two: *believe and love* (see 1 John 3:23). Jesus' commandments can't be added to Moses' because the Law wasn't allowed to be altered in any way (see Deuteronomy 4:2, John 1:17, Matthew 5:48, James 2:10, Galatians 3:10).

So we have to pick one: Moses or Jesus. Law or grace. 613 or 2.

We *love* Moses, we *respect* Moses, but his time ended at the Cross for all who will believe (see Hebrews 3:1-6, Romans 10:4, Galatians 2:19). The jots and tittles from the 613 are still there but only for unbelievers to realize they're failing miserably at *following* those jots and tittles. Law usage, from its inception, was meant to expose an unbeliever's need for grace (see Romans 5:20, 6:14, 1 Corinthians 15:56). It also reminds the believer of just how blessed we are to not have to follow it. It's like looking at an old ex who's making their new partner miserable; you've already been through that pain and now you're free (see Matthew 5:18, 1 Timothy 1:7-10, Galatians 3:12, Romans 7:1-4).

When we read the Bible and come across the word *commandment* we must discern: *Is this for me, according to the New Covenant, or for the Jews, according to the Old Covenant?* As we comprehend the difference, the Great Commission is quite simple.

To further our knowledge, there are two primary sections of the Great Commission we must pay close attention to in order to establish its foundation. I've underlined both:

> *And Jesus came and said to them, "All authority in heaven and on earth has been given to me. Go therefore and make disciples of all nations, baptizing them in the name of the Father and of the Son and of the Holy Spirit, teaching them to observe all that I have commanded you. And behold, I am with you always, to the end of the age." (Matthew 28:18-20)*

1. ***all nations*** – Not *just* the Jewish nation, but the entire world. This is the Abrahamic promise which was made before Israel and the Law was even formed.
2. ***teaching them to observe all that I have commanded you*** – Teach and observe all the *New Covenant* commandments and post-Cross realities *not* Moses' commandments.

Context, context, context!

We've already gone over Jesus' two new commandments, so what else were they to teach and observe? Some amazing, outstanding, and mind-blowing things!

- There's no distinction between Jew and Gentile, we're *all* a new creation in Christ! (Romans 10:12,20, Ephesians 3:6, Galatians 3:28, 2 Corinthians 5:17)
- Jesus is the Messiah foretold about in the Jews' own scriptures! (Genesis 3:15, Isaiah 53:5, John 5:39)

- There's no longer a holy geographical area on planet earth! *We* are now the holy place, the very house of God; walking, talking *temples* of His Spirit! (Acts 17:24, 1 Corinthians 6:19, Hebrews 3:3-5)
- Outside appearances mean nothing if our inside appearance isn't cleaned by faith in Christ! (Matthew 23:27, Acts 15:19, 1 Corinthians 6:11)
- The Cross was the final altar! There are no more bloody animal sacrifices left to be made for forgiveness, nor will Jesus ever die again! (John 19:30, Hebrews 1:3, 7:24-25, 10:1-29)
- Simply *believe* in God's Son to be saved! Yes, the demons believe too, they know who Christ is, but *they* are already damned to hell and can't receive forgiveness by faith! (John 1:12-13, 3:16-18, Ephesians 2:8-9)
- God's Spirit indwells us permanently, His ministry is to counsel us every moment of our lives! The Law is a ministry of death, which includes the Ten Commandments! It doesn't guide us, not even for morality! The Spirit of Jesus Christ does! (John 14:26, 16:13, 2 Corinthians 3:7-11)
- God's laws (lowercase and plural), as in, His very character, is now written on our hearts! Not the Law of Moses but the law of love! (Hebrews 8:11-13, 10:16, Romans 13:8-10, Galatians 5:14)

But wait, there's more!

- We are completely sanctified in our identity! Remember what sanctified means? HOLY! Our actions and attitudes are *being* sanctified *by* our holy identity, not the other way around! (Hebrews 10:10, Acts 20:32, Romans 12:2, James 1:4, 2 Peter 1:5-9)
- Our fellowship with God can never be broken because of the promise between the Father and Son made to one another at the Cross! (John 10:28, Hebrews 6:16-19, 2 Timothy 2:13)

- We *receive* forgiveness! We don't seek it, ask for it, or take it! Forgiveness is already *offered* to the unbelievers of humanity because God knows they need it! We simply open up our hands of faith and say, "Thank you," once, to receive it! (The word *receive* is used in the New Testament 150 to 200+ times depending on the translation! Wow!)
- Believers are complete, holy, pure, blameless, and free from all accusation of people and the enemy! (Colossians 1:22, 2:9-10, 2 Corinthians 5:21)
- We've received a new heart which is no longer wicked and sinful! (Ezekiel 36:26, Acts 15:9, Romans 6:17)

You thought I was done? No, not yet! Here's even *more* amazing New Covenant truths!

- We're *already* seated in heaven, spiritually, because we're already *in* Christ and Christ is *in* heaven! (John 14:20, Ephesians 2:6, 1 Corinthians 6:17)
- We're no longer called servants but family and friends! (John 15:15, 1 John 3:1, Hebrews 2:11)
- We don't *want* to sin and we'll prove this by sinning and being miserable or by living holy and feeling like a well-oiled machine! (Romans 7:20, 2 Peter 1:4, Galatians 5:22-23)
- Water baptism doesn't save, only spiritual baptism. If this weren't true then the gospel would be a water-works message. The fact is, there's not enough water in all the universe to wash away our sins. Only the blood of Christ can do this. Some people don't even have access to water. Water baptism is a *celebration,* like a birthday party; it's awesome, but not the actual event of life-giving birth. Any sinner can be

dunked in water, they must still repent of unbelief in Jesus' forgiveness to be placed inside of Him, once. That's what baptism means, "to place inside of." Water baptism is a *symbol* of spiritual baptism into Christ's very Spirit! We do this to celebrate! (Romans 6:3-4, 11:6, 1 Corinthians 1:14,17, 1 Peter 3:21, Colossians 3:3)

- It is *grace* that teaches us how to live upright, holy lives, not Law! Teach more grace and the results will be authentic saintly living! Teach more Law and sin will multiply like wet gremlins sitting at a buffet after midnight! (Titus 2:11-12, 1 Timothy 1:7, Hebrews 13:9, Romans 5:20, 6:14, 7:8,11, 1 Corinthians 15:56)
- Jesus will return in the same way He left! (Acts 1:9-11, 1 Thessalonians 4:16-18, Revelation 22:20)

There's exceedingly and abundantly *so* much more to teach and observe! This is what makes the Great Commission fun! We've only touched the tip of the iceberg of understanding what God has done for humanity through His Son!

Jesus commanded the disciples to communicate the New Covenant to the world when He gave the Great Commission, and don't get tripped up on the word *disciple.* He used this term because that's all they understood at the time. Disciple isn't used once in any of the epistles because after the truth began to spread about being one with God, through Paul's ministry, it became obsolete. A disciple is a follower, which anyone can have, yet Paul revealed we're not simply *following* a dead teacher's instructions. We're *combined* with the Spirit of the living Son of God! (See Colossians 1:27, 1 Corinthians 6:17, Hebrews 3:14).

One last thing. When Christ said to baptize people in the name of the Father, Son, and Holy Spirit, what *is* that name? *Jesus!* We must be placed *in* Him by faith in *His* very name, and no other!

So today, my friends, know this: The original disciples failed individually at fulfilling the Great Commission, at least at first. They didn't immediately do as Jesus said, it took them years before venturing out. Some didn't even leave until around AD70, being forced to, as Rome destroyed Jerusalem. Christ told them this would happen (see Matthew 24:2, Mark 13:2). Just like us, after first believing, they were still immature—perfect and holy, but babes. Their hometown was their bottle of milk and friendly converted Jews their blankets. As they hesitated on fulfilling the Great Commission what did Jesus do? He went out and recruited His most fierce enemy, Saul, to get the "all nations" thing started (see Acts 9:1-9, Romans 11:13). Saul, whose name later changed to Paul, could've rejected Christ on the road to Damascus. But even if he did, Jesus would've *still* found a way to get the truth out into the world, as was promised to Abraham 2,000 years earlier by God (see Genesis 17:4). This teaches us that the Great Commission is actually *Jesus'* mission *through* us! That is, for whosoever will make themselves available! That's you, friend. That's me too. We have a divine destiny. We will leave a legacy which lasts for eternity. God will work through our individual abilities and personalities just the same as a vine works through a branch. There's no pressure. There's only patience and encouragement. There's only love. We get to be ourselves, rest in Him, and enjoy this awesome relationship. As we do, we fulfill His Great Commission, naturally.

A prayer for you: *Father, today I'm extremely appreciative for being chosen to live a life on your planet. What a spectacular thing! Even more, I'm grateful that you chose to make your home in me, teaching me who you are and who you've remade me to be. Thank you, so much. Right now,*

I lift up all who are reading this, directly to you. Please let these wonderful people know the Great Commission is being fulfilled right on time, by you. They can relax as you work through them gracefully. Protect them, Father, as Jesus warned us that the truth of His grace is a sword which will divide because many will reject faith in Him. Strengthen them by the power of your Holy Spirit as they express your grace gently and respectfully to this fallen world. Give them comfort and continually remind them that you always finish what you start. Your commitment to us and to your plan is second to none. We're thankful and excited to be included in your Great Commission! In Jesus' mighty name I pray, amen!

Dear friend,

Thank you so much for spending time with me through this book. I hope I was able to bring you a sense of peace and confidence in knowing more about what Christ has truly done. My prayer is for you to grow into even deeper revelations of your identity as a believer. Lastly, it would mean the world to me if you'd leave a kind review on Amazon.com, Goodreads.com, Barnes & Noble's website, or wherever you've purchased this book. Your opinion is very important and encouraging to me. I always look forward to reading reviews.

May God continue to bless you greatly, with even more knowledge of His love for you through Jesus!

In Christ,
Matt

The Christian Identity, Volume 1: *Discovering What Jesus Has Truly Done to Us*

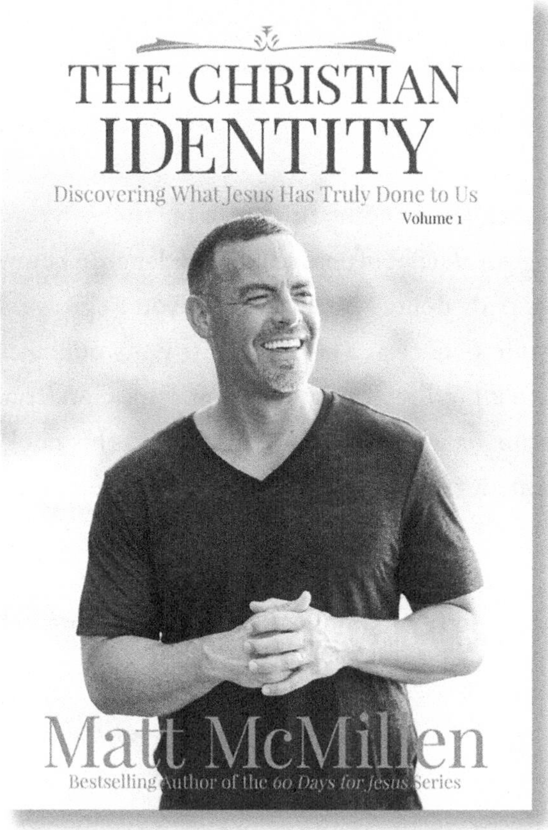

"Matt brilliantly explains the supernatural transformation that happens when we become believers in the finished work of the cross. His writing style makes this easy to understand as he answers some of the toughest questions that are on so many Christians' minds today." -*Amazon Customer*

The Christian Identity, Volume 2: *Discovering What Jesus Has Truly Done to Us*

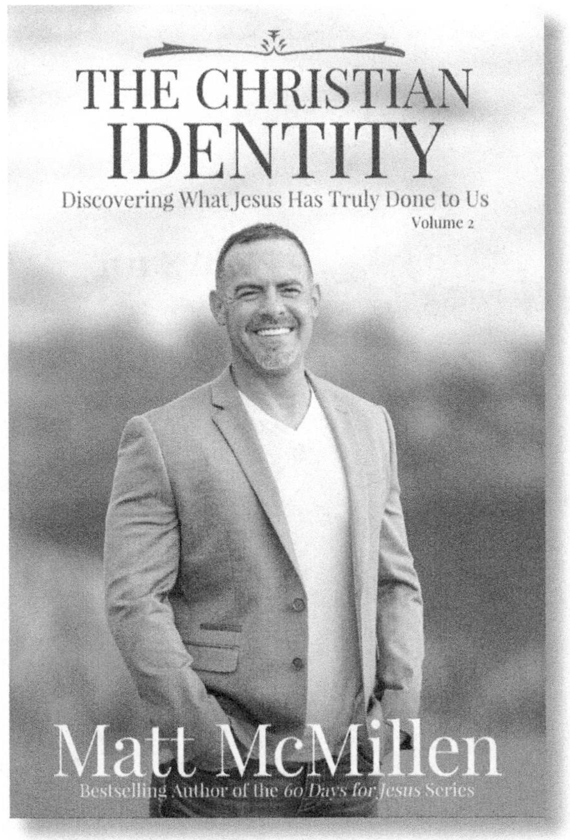

"Matt's writing is a breath of fresh air, bringing you into a freeing but solid sense of who you are in Christ. He cuts through religion and lifeless tradition that keeps people from experiencing the truth of Jesus which sets us free. He does this by pulling Scripture together contextually! A great read!" *-Amazon Customer*

60 Days for Jesus, Volume 1: *Understanding Christ Better, Two Months at a Time*

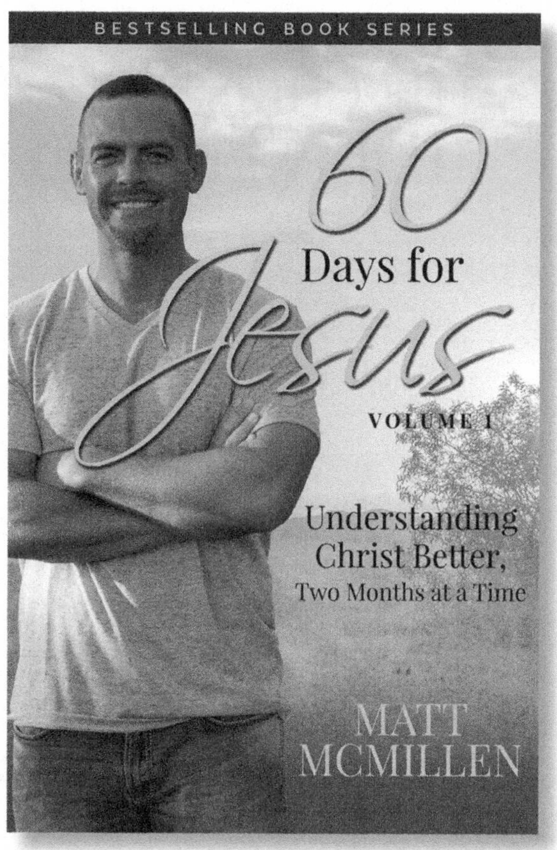

"I really like Matt's writing style. He makes understanding the gospel simple and real. I have found his daily devotions to be very helpful in guiding my walk with Christ. I highly recommend his book." -*Amazon Customer*

60 Days for Jesus, Volume 2: *Understanding Christ Better, Two Months at a Time*

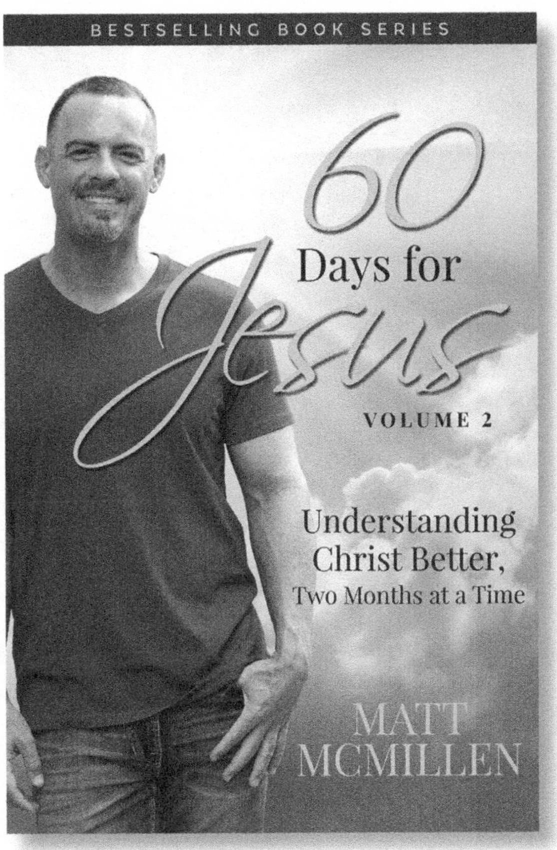

"This book is exactly what I needed to understand more about Jesus. I couldn't put it down. Thank you, Matt McMillen, for sharing your story to help strengthen others!" *-Amazon Customer*

60 Days for Jesus, Volume 3: *Understanding Christ Better, Two Months at a Time*

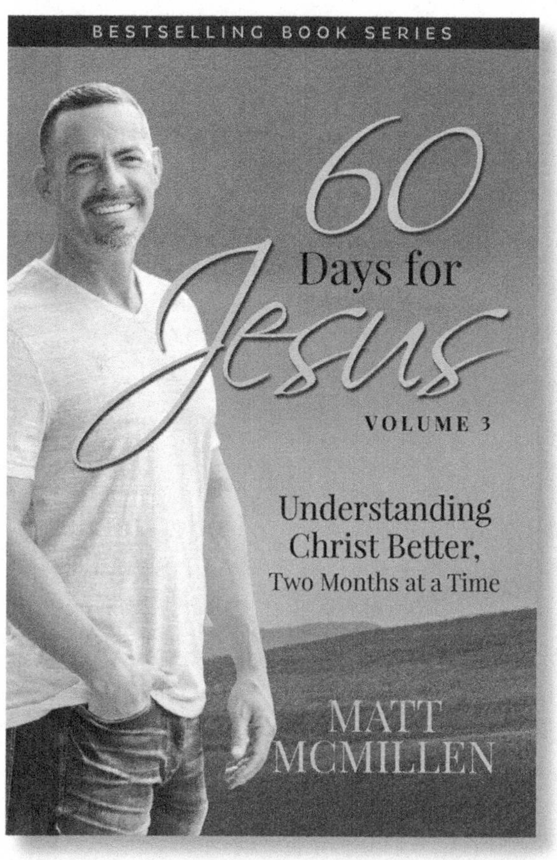

"Matt does an excellent job of providing clarity on many difficult issues every believer walks through on a daily basis. He does this by clearly articulating the scriptures to reveal the truth that really does set us free. This Volume, like the ones before, is an excellent devotional book to help any believer with their walk with God. Every page of this book is filled with the good news of God's unconditional love and grace. If you read one book this year, make it this one!" -*Amazon Customer*

True Purpose in Jesus Christ: *Finding the Relationship for Which You Were Made*

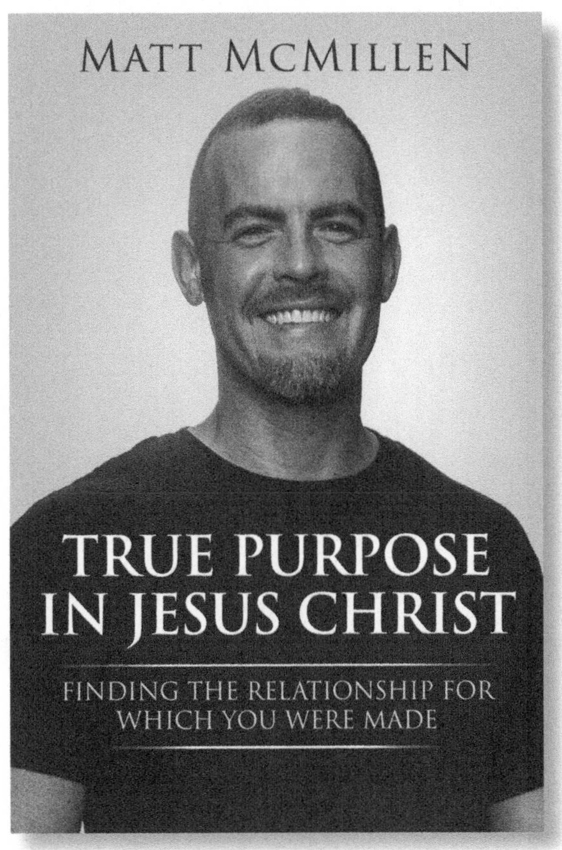

"One of the best books I've ever read! Matt's honesty about his life and what Jesus did to redeem him is amazing! He uses Scripture throughout his book to back up everything he talks about. I bought 20 books so I could share with the lost. Absolutely life changing! Thank you, Matt, for writing this book!" *-Amazon Customer*

Made in the USA
Monee, IL
23 December 2020

55207099R00125